Cliff Palace, the greatest known cliff dwelling

INDIANS
OF THE MESA VERDE

DON WATSON

Mesa Verde Museum Association

Mesa Verde National Park

Colorado

LITHOPRINTED IN THE UNITED STATES OF AMERICA BY
CUSHING - MALLOY, INC., ANN ARBOR, MICHIGAN, 1961

CONTENTS

Part One

PEOPLE OF THE MESA VERDE

Part Two

THE ARCHEOLOGICAL BACKGROUND

ILLUSTRATIONS

PART ONE

People of the Mesa Verde

1

ECHOS OF THE PAST

Under the arching roof of a tremendous cave stands a silent, empty city.

For almost seven centuries it has stood there looking out across the canyon toward the setting sun. Proudly, almost haughtily, it has resisted the heavy tread of those slow centuries. Like a giant with a shawl of everlasting stone pulled closely about its shoulders it has stood with unbowed head, an eternal monument to the intelligence and industry of its builders.

Almost seven centuries ago the people turned their backs on their proud city and walked away. All of the forces of nature seemed to be against them. The rains failed to fall; the springs ceased to flow. No corn grew in the fields. At last, weak from lack of food and water, and bewildered by the failure of the gods to answer their hysterical prayers they surrendered to the inevitable. Sadly they turned their backs on the once happy city and walked down the canyon, never to return.

Cliff Palace, the crowning glory of the Mesa Verde, was a silent, deserted city.

In spite of the protection offered by the cave Cliff Palace has suffered from the leveling forces of time. The owls and pack rats have been careless tenants and the lack of repair is evident. Some of the walls have cracked; a few have fallen. Foundations have slipped; roofs have disappeared. The once-bright plaster is peeling from the walls.

These minor changes have failed to dim the splendor of the largest of all cliff dwellings. From one end of the cave to the other stand unbroken lines of houses. Story upon story they rise to the very roof of the cave itself. On a still higher ledge, far up under the cave roof, stands a long row of small rooms where the people once stored their abundant supplies of grain. In some of the houses paintings are still bright on the walls; in others footprints of the people are still clearly evident in the

3

hard-packed clay floors. At each end of the cave is the trail which once led to the corn fields on the mesa top; below the cave is the trail that led to the bottom of the canyon.

In reality Cliff Palace has not changed a great deal since that day when its inhabitants disappeared. They walked away, it is true, but they are still there. You can see them if you close your eyes.

Unfortunate indeed, is he who views this ancient city and sees only the towering walls. Unfortunate because the stones are the least important part. Cliff Palace is really built of the hopes and desires, the joys and sorrows of an industrious people. It is not a cold, empty city for it is still warm with the emotions of its builders. In each fingerprint and tool mark lie the prayers of a young couple for a home filled with children and happiness. Each storage bin is chinked with a farmer's prayers for a bountiful harvest. In each plastered kiva wall is an ancient priest's reverence for his gods. A pot is not just a piece of baked clay: it is an ancient potter's moulded prayer for beauty and strength. Each solid wall is a testimony of success; each shattered human bone, each broken jar is an admission of defeat.

Cliff Palace stands today as a monument to the ancient people of the Mesa Verde. For many centuries they occupied the great, green mesa and finally, almost in its center, they built their greatest city. Certainly it was their outstanding architectural achievement but it is only one of many hundreds of ruins which stand in silent testimony to the skills of an industrious people.

For over a thousand years the Indians enjoyed the security and bounty of the Mesa Verde. In the beginning their culture was simple but as the centuries passed they progressed steadily without taking a backward step. Finally they reached the highest point of their development and for the brief century during which they occupied the cliff dwellings they enjoyed the fruits of their long struggle. Then catastrophe came and in a short time they were gone.

The complete archeological wealth of the Mesa Verde will never be known. The great mesa, which rises high above the surrounding country, measures fifteen miles from north to

Top. The north rim of the mesa rises 2000 feet above the valley
Bottom. The flat mesa top is cut by a score of rugged canyons

south and twenty miles from east to west. Its flat top, sloping gently to the south, is cut by a score of rugged canyons and access to the remote areas is difficult. The ruins are often hard to find and many will never be discovered. In the days of discovery, as we shall see in the next chapter, the early explorers entered almost every cliff dwelling but they left few records. In recent times it is doubtful if one-third of the cliff dwellings have been entered and probably no living person has been in one hundred of them.

The ruins on the mesa tops far outnumber the cliff dwellings but most of them are difficult to find. Earth and vegetation have covered them, often completely, and intensive search does not reveal all. This wealth of mesa-top ruins is indicated by a recent survey of a small portion of one mesa. Careful search of an area of only three square miles revealed over three hundred ruins.

In 1906, one-half of the great mesa was set aside as Mesa Verde National Park in order that the ruins might be preserved for all time and made accessible to visitors. Cliff Palace and some of the other cliff dwellings have been excavated and out on the mesa tops ruins of earlier types have been excavated to complete the archeological story. In the nearby museum are to be seen the things which have been found in the ruins. Displayed in their chronological order they tell the story of the ancient inhabitants of the Mesa Verde.

It is a fascinating story of a vanished people. For endless centuries they dominated the Mesa Verde, passing through higher and higher stages of culture. When an unendurable calamity forced them to leave they left behind abundant evidence of their skill and industry. With the care they now receive Cliff Palace, Spruce Tree House, Sun Temple and the innumerable other ruins will stand forever as monuments to the skill of their ancient builders.

Mesa Verde National Park was created to preserve the works of those prehistoric people. Slow, silent centuries have spread a cloak of mystery over it and visitors should come with open minds, prepared to hear an absorbing story of a strange people. Complete enjoyment and understanding come only to the visitor who is able to leave his modern self behind, momentarily, and live and think in terms of the past.

2

DISCOVERY

After the cliff dwellings were deserted by the Pueblo Indians late in the thirteenth century they stood, unmolested by man, for many hundreds of years. The owls and pack rats took them over and enjoyed their security, but from all evidence it was many centuries before men again entered the caves.

The Indians themselves may have intended to return when conditions became normal again but they never came back. There is no evidence that farming Indians ever lived in the Mesa Verde after its desertion by the ancient people. Other Indians came but they were hunters and they seem to have shunned the silent cave cities.

A couple of centuries after Mesa Verde was deserted an important event took place, an event that was to have a strange effect on it at a later date.

America was rediscovered!

Fifteen thousand years after the Indians discovered the continent from the west, white men entered it from the east. A new people blundered into the western hemisphere that had so long belonged to the Indians.

The newcomers were a greedy lot and they began to stretch acquisitive fingers in all directions. Mexico was colonized and tales of wealth among the Indians to the north led the Spaniards into the Southwest. In 1540, Coronado was only 150 miles from the Mesa Verde but he turned away. Other Spaniards came nearer and nearer until at last, in the year 1776, they were at the base of the great green mesa.

On August 10, 1776, only thirty-seven days after the signing of the Declaration of Independence, Escalante, a Spanish priest, camped in the very shadow of the Mesa Verde. It seems almost incredible that at a time when the colonists along the Atlantic seaboard knew nothing of the vast wilderness beyond the first range of mountains, Escalante and his men were here in the land of the cliff dwellings. Seeking a short route to Monterey,

9

on the Pacific Coast, they had journeyed northwest from Santa Fe. At last, on August 10, 1776, they camped by a small stream at the base of the La Plata Mountains.

In his diary Escalante wrote:

"August 10. Father Fray Francisco Atanasio awoke troubled by a rheumatic fever which he had felt in his face and head since the day before, and it was desirable that we make camp here until he should be better, but the continuous rains, the inclemency of the weather, and the great dampness of the place forced us to leave it. Going north, and having traveled a little more than half a league, we turned to the northwest, went on a league and then swung west through valleys of very beautiful timber and abundant pasturage, roses, and various other flowers. After going two leagues we were again caught in a very heavy rain. Father Fray Francisco Atanasio became worse and the road impassable, and so, having traveled with great difficulty two more leagues to the west, we had to camp on the bank of the first of the two little rivers which form the San Lazaro, otherwise called Rio de los Mancos. The pasturage continues in great abundance. Today four and a half leagues."

The small stream beside which Escalante camped that night is still called the Mancos. Only a few miles below his camping place it cuts directly into the Mesa Verde. The former inhabitants of the cliff dwellings had known it well. It had failed them during the great drouth. And now, on August 10, 1776, exactly 500 years after the beginning of that drouth which had caused them to leave the Mesa Verde, Escalante, a man of a new race, camped beside the Mancos, only a few miles from the empty ruins of the cliff dwellings.

Without doubt he saw the great mesa, the Mesa Verde, for it looms high above the Mancos Valley. But he turned away; he was seeking the sea to the west.

During the following three-quarters of a century many other Spaniards must have seen the Mesa Verde for there was much exploration in the region. Sometime during this period the mesa was given a Spanish name – Mesa Verde – the "green table." The Spaniard who named it is unknown. Possibly he named it after climbing to its summit for from the valley below it is not so evident that the top is flat and eternally green.

Could it be that he even saw the cliff dwellings and we have failed to find the record in the musty archives of Mexico or Spain? No, probably not. We must consider that the cliff dwellings were still unseen by modern man.

In 1848, the Mesa Verde, although still unknown, passed from Mexican to American ownership. Slowly the new owners drew nearer. The date of discovery of the now aged cliff dwellings was close at hand.

The first known mention of the Mesa Verde was made in the year 1859. In that year an exploring expedition set out from Santa Fe, under the leadership of Captain J. N. Macomb, to explore certain territory in what is now the State of Utah. Serving as geologist for this expedition was Professor J. S. Newberry and in his geological report he wrote:

"Between the Rio de la Plata and the Rio de los Mancos we skirted the base of the extreme southern point of the Sierra de la Plata. These mountains terminate southward in a long slope, which falls down to a level of about 7500 feet above the sea, forming a plateau which extends southward to the San Juan, the Mesa Verde, to which I shall soon have occasion again to refer."

Farther on in his report he adds:

"To obtain a just conception of the enormous denudation which the Colorado Plateau has suffered, no better point of view could possibly be selected than that of the summit of the Mesa Verde. The geologist here has, it seems to me, satisfactory proof of the proposition I have before made...."

From the manner in which he spoke of the Mesa Verde it is very evident Professor Newberry voiced a name that was in common usage. This was true also of all the rivers and mountains mentioned in his report. Their names indicate the Spaniards had done a very thorough job of christening the landmarks of the region.

From Newberry's report it is also evident that he climbed to the summit of the Mesa Verde. His description indicates he must have scaled one of the high points along the northern rim, possibly Park Point, the highest of all. He merely climbed to the summit, feasted his geological eyes on the thrilling view over 16,000 square miles of wilderness, and descended. He was only a few miles from the ruins but he failed to suspect their presence. He does deserve credit, however, for the first known mention of the Mesa Verde and for the earliest modern ascent to its summit.

The first American settlers entered the Mesa Verde region about 1870. Miners, farmers, trappers, cattlemen, even bandits, came pouring into the Mancos Valley and found it to their liking. None of them had ever heard of, or would have been interested in the ruins. To them the past was dead and forgotten; they were looking ahead. They were interested only in taming the wilderness and in keeping their scalps firmly attached to their heads.

At that time the entire region was terrorized by the Ute Indians. Naturally a war-like group they were goaded into a frenzy by the loss of their hunting grounds and they made life miserable for the whites. Adventurous miners and trappers were slain; farming settlements lived in constant fear of the merciless warriors. The situation became acute and soldiers finally were sent in to hold the Utes in check.

To the settlers the Indians were simple hazards to be expected in the conquest of the wilderness. They were merely to be brushed aside. If they resented the brushing process, if they showed a tendency to resist the loss of their ancient tribal homes, it was very unfortunate — for the Indians. The persuasive little leaden pellets of the settlers convinced one Ute after another that it was wrong to resent the loss of homes and hunting grounds. The remnants of the tribe sought refuge in natural strongholds, especially in strongholds where there was nothing desired by the whites.

One of these natural strongholds was the Mesa Verde. Its warm lower canyons had long been the winter home of bands of Utes and they were familiar with every nook and cranny in it. The deep, narrow canyons and high mesas offered sanctuary to the oppressed Indians. The settlers in the Mancos Valley respected this wilderness stronghold and it remained a place of mystery to them. From the time of Professor Newberry's climb to the summit in 1859, we have no definite record of white men entering the Mesa Verde until 1874.

In that year a small party of explorers ventured into the forbidding canyons of the great mesa. The young government far off to the east was endeavoring to learn the extent and nature of its newly acquired possessions in the far west. Small surveying parties were being sent into all parts of the vast unknown land. One of these parties drifted down from the north and entered the Mesa Verde region in the year 1874. In charge of the party was Mr. W. H. Jackson, photographer for the U. S. Geological and Geographical Survey. Jackson and his men were not interested in the Mesa Verde, in fact they had no knowledge of its existence until men whom they encountered in some of the mining camps began to tell of a great tableland filled with mysterious ruins.

Jackson was intrigued and although he had little faith in the strange rumors, he decided to explore the Mesa Verde. His guide on the expedition was a garrulous miner named John Moss who claimed to have first-hand knowledge of the ruins. This chapter in the story of the Mesa Verde is extremely vague. There is no doubt that before the time of Jackson's expedition some of the settlers knew of the Mesa Verde ruins. How much they knew is uncertain. Some of the early prospectors or hunters may actually have seen them. The Mancos Canyon afforded a natural avenue for travel through the Mesa Verde and in spite of the Ute danger, the intrepid adventurers may have used it occasionally. If they did, they could hardly have failed to see the many ruins that clung to the faces of the cliffs far above the river.

On the other hand, knowledge of the Mesa Verde ruins may have come from the Indians. In a little while we will see a friendly Ute Indian giving the white men their first knowledge of Cliff Palace. Perhaps John Moss and the other miners heard of the existence of the ruins from friendly Utes or Navahos.

At any rate, John Moss knew that there were ruins in the Mesa Verde, and in September, 1874, he led Jackson into the Mancos Canyon. The first night they camped on the banks of the river in the heart of the Mesa Verde. A century earlier Escalante had camped a few miles farther up the same stream. Six centuries earlier Indian maidens had filled their water jars from it.

No cliff dwellings had been seen and the men were beginning to lose faith in the stories of their guide. As dusk was settling over the canyon, the men stood about their campfire.

"Moss," one of the men questioned, "where are those ruins that you have been telling us about?"

"Right up there," Moss replied, with a swing of his arm that took in the whole out-of-doors.

Unimpressed, the men stepped away from the campfire and began to scan the cliffs above. In the bottom of the canyon they stood in the gathering shadows of twilight but far above the cliffs were lighted by the last dying embers of the setting sun. Suddenly the men saw what John Moss had not even suspected when he had said, "Right up there."

In the topmost cliff was a cave and in it, standing out in bold relief against the shadowy background, were small stone houses. Moss was right — there was a ruin "up there."

In spite of the growing darkness the men scrambled up the canyon walls. Just as total darkness fell, two of them entered the little cliff dwelling. It was the earliest known discovery of a Mesa Verde cliff dwelling by white men.

The next morning Jackson and his men returned to the ruin and photographed it. Two-Story Cliff House they named it because of a splendidly-built, two-story structure it contained. Excitedly they climbed about the small village, poking into every dark corner. In the debris of the cluttered rooms they found things that aided them in their wild speculations about the vanished people; pottery, corn cobs, stone tools — the Mesa Verde was beginning to give up its secrets.

Today Two-Story Cliff House still clings to the face of its cliff. It has changed little since Jackson saw it and few men have entered it since that fatal day when the Indians left it behind.

Long ago the people of Two-Story House were neighbors of the people of Cliff Palace, the great cliff dwelling toward which we are moving. To them it must have been a metropolis, a great city, the largest they ever knew. It took only an hour for them to trot up the canyon to the larger community. Often the men of the little village must have slung their prized possessions

Two Story Cliff House, discovered by Mr. W. H. Jackson, in 1874

15

over their shoulders and set out for Cliff Palace on trading and gambling expeditions. It was "big town" to them.

When Jackson was at Two-Story Cliff House he was very near Cliff Palace but he did not see the larger ruin. If he had gone only four miles up the nearest side canyon, he would have found the amazing structure. But he was satisfied with the discovery of Two-Story Cliff House and other small ruins and a narrowly-averted clash with a band of Utes sent him scuttling down the Mancos Canyon and out of the Mesa Verde to safety. Cliff Palace was still unknown but the threat of discovery was coming nearer.

One of the early settlers in the Mancos Valley was Mr. B. K. Wetherill, a rancher. In the eighties he and his five sons were living on a large ranch at the foot of the Mesa Verde. It was a typical pioneer family but in one respect the Wetherills were very different from their neighbors. Throughout all of their years of residence in the valley they had been friendly with the Utes. Instead of persecuting them as so many of the settlers did, they befriended the helpless Indians who were rapidly losing the lands they regarded as their own. Indians were welcome at the Wetherill ranch and the bonds of friendship grew strong.

As a result of this friendship, the Wetherills began to run their cattle in the Mancos Canyon. At last, white men were welcome in the vast stronghold of the Utes. Deeper and deeper they penetrated into the network of canyons.

As they worked with their cattle the Wetherills began to notice tiny houses standing in caves on the faces of the cliffs. They even climbed to them and as they explored the little villages their interest and curiosity mounted. The houses were merely small stone rooms, evidently built in the caves for security. In the houses the boys found things the ancient inhabitants had left behind, even the remains of the people themselves. They speculated on the origin of their finds but there seemed to be no answers. The objects found seemed to have no actual value so they spent little time in the ancient buildings. Their cattle could not be neglected for the tiny houses in the cliffs.

An interesting tale came to the Wetherill brothers' ears when they became acquainted with a Ute Indian named Acowitz.

In some of the canyons, he told them, were cliff dwellings that were much larger than any they had seen. There was one cliff dwelling that was the largest of all. When he showed them how large it was and how many rooms it contained they were quite sure he could not be believed. No cliff dwelling could be so large.

Acowitz persisted in his claims. Time after time he told the Wetherills of the ruin that was the largest in the Mesa Verde. Dubious but interested, the boys began to watch the cliffs whenever their search for cattle took them into new canyons.

At last Al Wetherill thought he saw it.

He was following the bottom of a canyon in which none of the boys had ever been. Far above, in the highest cliff, he saw the arched roof of an enormous cave. Through the tops of the trees Al thought he saw houses; he could not be sure. Anxious to reach camp before darkness came he did not climb up to investigate. The boys began to consider the claims of Acowitz with less doubt. The cave seemed to exist; perhaps it did contain the largest cliff dwelling of all.

The following winter two of the Wetherill brothers, Richard and Alfred, and their brother-in-law, Charlie Mason, were again in the Mesa Verde with their cattle. Day after day they watched them, often riding the high mesa trails in search of strays. As they rode they remembered the story of Acowitz and the cave Al had seen. Before the winter was over they intended to find it.

One snowy December day in 1888, Richard Wetherill and Charlie Mason rode their horses up out of the Mancos Canyon and began to follow the trail of some stray cattle northward across the mesa top. Snow lay deep on the ground. Soft flakes filled the air. Silently the two forced their way through the heavy growth of pinon and juniper trees. Only the thud of the horses' feet and the creak of saddle leather broke the silence. Near the edge of a canyon the growth thinned out and they finally rode out into the open.

"Charlie, look at that!" cried Richard, pointing across the canyon.

In the opposite wall was a tremendous cave. Filling it from one end to the other, and rising even to its vaulted roof, was a silent city of stone. No snow fell on the ancient city. No storm had touched it through all the centuries. It seemed as eternal as the ageless cliff that protected it.

Framed by the magnificent cave, a thin veil of snowflakes drawn across its face, the silent city cast a spell over the two cowboys. In all that vast wilderness there was no sound but the soft hiss of the snowflakes and the throbbing of the boys' hearts. Speechless, they sat in their saddles.

At last one of the horses stirred and the spell was broken.

As the first flush of discovery passed, the two boys began to search for a way to enter the ruin. Riding around the heads of two small canyons they were soon above their goal. An ancient trail led down the cliff. Breathless with excitement, they walked into the cave and, as Charles Mason later recounted:

"We spent several hours going from room to room, and picked up several articles of interest, among them a stone axe with the handle still on it. There were also parts of several human skeletons scattered about."

Once again the great cliff dwelling knew the touch of man. Six centuries after the despairing Indians deserted their home, two flushed, happy men walked into it. A new era had dawned, one that would see strange happenings in the Mesa Verde.

Excitedly the two cowboys scrambled about the ruin, prying into every corner, appraising the many strange things they found. Acowitz had been right; it was tremendous. They could never hope to find another ruin as large. Throughout its entire length the cave was full of houses; simple stone rooms with small, high doorways and few windows. Here and there among the houses were mysterious circular, subterranean rooms that the boys could not understand. At the south end of the cave was a four-story structure that touched the cave roof; in the third-story room was a beautiful painting in red and white. At the north end a terraced structure also rose to the cave roof; in it was some of the best masonry in the entire cave. On an upper ledge at the back of the cave was a long row of smaller rooms. In them the boys found corn cobs, tassels and shucks. Under flat rocks, where rats had not found them, were a few grains of corn and some brown beans. Instantly the boys knew the ancient people had been farmers.

In the center of the cave was a graceful round tower. Every stone in it was carefully rounded to fit the curve of the wall and the entire tower tapered uniformly toward the top. In the tower was the finest stone axe the boys ever found. But the use of the tower puzzled them.

The ruin was in a sad state of repair. Roofs had fallen; walls had partially crumbled. Courts and passageways were choked with fallen stones, adobe mortar and broken roof beams. Rat nests filled the darker corners and a mantle of dust and cobwebs lay over all. Out of this jumble the once-proud city raised an unbowed head. Only minor parts had fallen. The greater part of it remained as the Indians had left it. The crumbled parts spoke of age and the forces of decay; the unbroken walls gave mute evidence of the skill of a vanished people.

In order to see the great ruin as it was on the day of discovery we must go again to Charles Mason's description, published in the Denver Post in 1917, for, because of its condition, he developed a strange theory.

"The final tragedy of the cliff dwellers probably occurred at Cliff Palace. There is scarcely room to doubt that the place withstood an extended siege. In the entire building only two timbers were found by us. All of the joists on which floors and roofs were laid had been wrenched out. These timbers are built into the walls and are difficult to remove, even the little willows on which the mud roofs and upper floors are laid were carefully taken out. No plausible reason for this has been advanced except that it was used as fuel.

"Another strange circumstance is that so many of their valuable possessions were left in the rooms and covered with the clay of which the roofs and upper floors were made, not to mention many of the walls broken down in tearing out the timbers. It would seem that the intention was to conceal their valuables, so their enemies might not secure them, or perhaps the people were in such despair that property was not considered.

"There were many human bones scattered about, as though several people had been killed and left unburied. Had Cliff Palace been abandoned, as has been suggested, and the timbers used in other buildings, all movable articles of value would have been taken away, instead of being covered and much of it broken and destroyed unnecessarily.

"It seems to me that there can be no doubt that the Cliff Dwellers were exterminated by their more savage and warlike neighbors, the men being killed and the women being adopted into the tribe of the conquerors, though in some cases migrations may have become necessary as a result of drouth or pressure from outside tribes."

While it would be difficult to prove Charles Mason's theory that "The final tragedy of the cliff dwellers probably occurred at Cliff Palace," some of his other ideas were sound. The results of many years of intensive research by leading scientists show that he did a shrewd bit of forecasting when he suggested that "migrations may have become necessary as a result of drouth or pressure from outside tribes."

After exploring Cliff Palace for several hours, the two cowboys, flushed with excitement over their discovery, decided to search for more ruins. Climbing out of the great cave, they mounted their horses and, in order to cover more territory, separated. Mason rode off to the north, while Wetherill went to the north and west. Mason's search was fruitless but to Richard Wetherill goes credit for the second discovery of the day. After a short ride he came to a small canyon and, seeing no ruins along its western wall, rode around the head of the canyon and turned back to examine the eastern cliffs.

Immediately the discovery came. Within a hundred yards of the head of the canyon was a long, low cave and in it was another great cliff dwelling. While not as large as Cliff Palace, it was in a better state of preservation. This ruin, later named Spruce Tree House, has since proved to be the best-preserved large cliff dwelling in the Mesa Verde.

Night was approaching so Richard made no attempt to enter the ruin. Turning back, he met Mason at a prearranged spot near Cliff Palace and they camped for the night.

The following morning the two men set off to explore the ruin Richard had seen. Misjudging their direction, they turned too far to the west and within a short time found themselves on the rim of one of the deepest canyons of the Mesa Verde. The ruin for which they had been searching had eluded them but instead of being disappointed, the two men were elated. At the foot of the cliff, almost under their feet, was a third great cliff dwelling.

This ruin was not as large as the two they had found the day before but it was much larger than any they had seen previously. In the center of the cliff dwelling was a tower, the tallest in the Mesa Verde, and because of this outstanding structure, the cowboys named the ruin Square Tower House.

For a time the two men sat on their horses, looking down on the ruin and discussing their discoveries. During the past few years they had seen many small cliff dwellings in the Mancos Canyon and in other canyons to the south. Now they had moved to the north and in two days had discovered three cliff dwellings that dwarfed all the others. Off to the north and west they could see still more canyons and they felt quite sure that countless ruins were yet to be found. The importance of their discoveries was all too appraent, so without pausing to search for more ruins, or for the cattle they had originally sought, they hurried back to the town of Mancos and spread the news of what they had found.

Upon hearing of the amazing discoveries, John Wetherill decided to investigate for himself. With three companions he made his way to Cliff Palace. Near the south end of the ruin, just back of the painted tower, one of the subterranean rooms was in perfect condition except that the roof was missing. After cleaning it out carefully, the boys stretched a canvas over it and the room served as their home for a month.

It was a strange use for the ancient room. Six hundred years earlier it had been a sacred ceremonial room, a kiva, where reverent priests had conducted their ceremonies. Now it was merely a living place for men of a different race. The cowboys built their fire in the same firepit where the priests had built theirs centuries earlier. They stored their food and possessions on the same ledges where the priests had kept their ceremonial things. They slept on the floor, exactly where the tired priests had slept during their long ceremonies. The boys had no knowledge that they were profaning a place of worship. It was not until many years later that they learned they had lived in a kiva, one of the ceremonial rooms of the ancient people.

During the month they spent in the ruin John Wetherill and his three friends searched endlessly for the things they knew were buried under the debris. In the houses, under the dust and fallen roofs, they found the utensils and tools the women had once used. In the kivas they found the ceremonial paraphernalia and tools of the men. Everywhere were the objects that had been used in the daily life of the people. It became evident that the ancient people had deserted their homes, leaving in them the things they were unable to carry. Perhaps they had intended to return and had left most of their possessions behind.

Far back in the cave where there were no buildings the most exciting discovery was made. In this part of the cave the roof was too low for houses so the inhabitants had used it for a trash room and as a roost for their flocks of domesticated turkeys.

As the cowboys dug through the accumulated trash they suddenly found themselves face-to-face with the ancient Indians. For some strange reason fourteen bodies had been buried there in the trash. Natural processes had mummified them so perfectly that in some the normal expression of the faces seemed to be preserved. It was a thrilling discovery for there, except for two things, were the Indians. In only two ways did the mummies differ from the cowboys themselves. Only the moisture and the spark of life were missing. If they could have restored those two things the men would have found themselves confronted with the actual builders of the cliff dwelling they were exploring.

Centuries earlier sorrowing relatives had buried them there in the back of the cave. The dry earth and trash drew the moisture from the flesh and, finally, only bones and dried tissues remained. Nothing was missing except the spark of life and the moisture. Everything else was in place; the bones, flesh, skin, eyes, internal organs; all were there, only very, very dry. Long hair still hung about the shoulders of the mummies and in it were the mummies of ancient lice which had once formed a happy population.

John Wetherill found fourteen mummies in Cliff Palace. It was a fitting climax to his first venture in archeology. Of the five Wetherill brothers, John was the one who developed the greatest interest in the ancient cultures. For many years after his first work in Cliff Palace he was actively engaged in exploring the Mesa Verde and nearby regions and making their features known to the world.

It was a strange month the four cowboys spent in Cliff Palace in that winter of 1888-89. In the midst of a silent snow-covered wilderness they lived in and explored an ancient city that was unknown to the civilized world. Centuries earlier it had sheltered the Indians. Now it sheltered the newcomers. Untouched by wind and snow they pried into the secrets of the ancient people.

Within a short time after discovery the great ruin received its name. Some of the early writers gave Richard Wetherill credit for christening it but in later years John Wetherill gave the credit to Charles Mason. In all probability we shall never know who deserves the credit but we may feel sure the name indicates the feelings those early explorers had about the greatest of all cliff dwellings.

Cliff Palace was the name they gave it, an inspiring name for the greatest structure the Mesa Verde people ever built. It is not especially appropriate for the great ruin was never a palace. Instead, it was a small city, the dwelling place of hundreds of people. But the name was the choice of the men who first explored it and it reflects their feelings toward the ancient structure.

Now we must pause for a moment. The story of the discovery of the cliff dwellings would not be complete if we were to go further without admitting that there are some uncertainties. Many years after the events we have just witnessed were a matter of record, other men came forward with claims that they had seen Cliff Palace before 1888. Even the various Wetherill brothers did not agree entirely in their stories about the discovery of the ruins. As a result, there is a certain amount of confusion concerning the events of those early days.

But the two events we have just witnessed can be accepted without the slightest doubt. Jackson was in Two-Story Cliff

House in 1874, and Charles Mason and Richard Wetherill were in Cliff Palace in 1888. No one has ever questioned the claims of these men.

Jackson was travelling with a scientific party sent out by the government. He photographed Two-Story Cliff House and other small cliff dwellings in the Mancos Canyon and in the following year published the pictures and descriptions of the ruins in a scientific report. So to Jackson goes credit for the discovery of the first small cliff dwellings of the Mesa Verde. If John Moss, who was Jackson's guide, or other early explorers were in the ruins before 1874, no record has come down to us.

It is equally certain that Charles Mason and Richard Wetherill were in Cliff Palace in 1888, for they announced their discovery immediately. The account which has been given here has come directly from written records left by Charles Mason and John Wetherill, and from personal interviews with the two men.

In 1935, Mason visited the Mesa Verde for the last time. In spite of his 74 years he was active and alert and the events of the early days were clear in his mind. We drove along the canyon rims and without hesitation he pointed out the cliff from which he and Richard Wetherill had first seen Cliff Palace. For an hour we sat in the sun as he recalled the events of that day, December 18, 1888, when he and Richard had sat there on their horses, gazing in amazement at the great ruin.

"We had heard of Cliff Palace before we saw it," he said. "A Ute Indian, named Acowitz, had told us about it and we had always hoped to find it. The Utes were afraid of the ruins because of the spirits of the old people that they believed were in them. If we wanted to keep the Utes out of our camp we just put a skull up on a stick and they wouldn't come near."

Remembering the problems they had with their cattle, he added, "Hunting cattle in those days was no easy job. They were as wild as deer and the country was rough. Once we spent a week chasing them and all we got back to town was an old cow and her calf. We shot lots of them like deer and packed the meat out."

In 1932, John Wetherill visited the Mesa Verde. As we strolled through Cliff Palace he told of the month he and his three friends had spent there in 1888-89. He pointed out the kiva where they had lived, the spot where the beautiful stone axe had been found and the place where they had discovered the fourteen mummies. He recalled that all of the roofs had been torn out, just as Charles Mason said, and he remembered that they had found more baskets in Cliff Palace than in any other cliff dwelling.

Then, pointing across the canyon, he said, "That's where Richard and Charley were when they first saw Cliff Palace." The bold cliff at which he pointed is called Sun Point today, and it was from this same point that Mason said he and Richard Wetherill first saw Cliff Palace.

It is quite true that other men have claimed they were in Cliff Palace before 1888. Not a shred of documentary evidence has been found to support these claims, however, so credit for being the first modern men to enter the greatest of all cliff dwellings goes to Charles Mason and Richard Wetherill.

During the years that followed the discovery of Cliff Palace, the Wetherills and other men discovered hundreds of cliff dwellings in the canyons of the Mesa Verde. They found, also, that the mesa tops were dotted with additional hundreds of ruins. As a result of these discoveries the fame of the Mesa Verde spread and within a short time many men were digging in the ruins.

The period following 1888 is the sad chapter in the history of the Mesa Verde. From the very beginning it was apparent that digging in the ruins was a profitable business. The Wetherills sold their first collection for $3000 and the word spread that artifacts from the ruins had actual cash value. Charles Mason indicated this only too well in his article published in the Denver Post on July 1, 1917. The article was signed by four of the Wetherills and without doubt gives a fairly accurate picture of what happened in the Mesa Verde following the discovery of the ruins.

In referring to their second expedition Mason wrote, "This time we went at it in a more business-like manner. Our previous work had been carried out more to satisfy our own curiosity than for any other purpose but this time it was a business proposition." And in referring to a still later expedition Mason stated, "In spite of the fact that all of the cliff dwellings had been worked over two or three times, we succeeded in making a very good showing."

The Wetherills themselves took a number of collections of artifacts from the cliff dwellings. Most of these collections are now in museums and since the Wetherills kept notes on their findings the material has real scientific value. In 1891, Baron Gustav Nordenskiold, a young Swedish archeologist, excavated in a score of the cliff dwellings and took a splendid collection back to his homeland. Soon after his return home Nordenskiold died and the collection was sold to a museum in Finland, where it rests uneasily today. In addition to the Wetherills and Nordenskiold, many other men worked in the ruins and they probably carried away an equal amount of material.

As a result of all this early work the ruins were well cleaned out before the area was made a national park. A number of cliff dwellings have been excavated by archeologists in recent times and little material of any importance has been found in them.

Even though the Mesa Verde could only be reached by a thirty mile horseback trip, it was visited by a surprising number of people in those early years. Some came only to see the ruins but many came to dig and on the return trip the packs often bulged with things taken from the ruins. Priceless artifacts which had so long been unmolested were thoughtlessly carried away.

As a result of these visits, however, the fame of the Mesa Verde grew and finally public sentiment came to its aid. Gradually there developed a realization that the ruins should be preserved for all time and made accessible to all people.

The first effort toward this appears to have been made in 1886, even before the discovery of Cliff Palace and the other large cliff dwellings. In that year a group of Denver people called attention to the need for a national park to preserve the ruins of the Mesa Verde. Five years later the Colorado General Assembly addressed a memorial to the Congress and in 1894, two petitions were sent to the Congress urging that a part of the Mesa Verde be preserved as a national park.

As the years passed, the agitation continued but little was accomplished. In 1897, however, the attention of the Colorado Federation of Women's Clubs was directed to the problem and a committee of fourteen women was appointed to spearhead the fight. Three years later the committee was expanded into the Colorado Cliff Dwellings Association, an incorporated organization dedicated to the struggle for the preservation of the ruins.

With grim determination the women worked, both with officials in Washington and the Ute Indians whose reservation included the Mesa Verde. After years of disappointments their efforts were crowned with success for on June 29, 1906, the Congress passed a bill creating Mesa Verde National Park.

At last, after six hundred empty years, the cliff dwellings were again in the care of men who were interested in their well-being. These men were of a different race and their feelings toward the cliff dwellings were far different from those of the people who had built them. To the ancient people the cave structures had meant home and security. To the new caretakers they were a milestone in the story of mankind and as such they should be preserved for all time.

3

LIFE IN ANCIENT TIMES

In a little while we are going to do a very strange thing.

We are, first of all, going to go back seven centuries to the year 1268 A.D. Then we will climb down the trail and stroll into Cliff Palace. Somewhere near the center of the town we will find a comfortable seat on the roof of one of the houses. And for a year we will sit there, quietly and comfortably, watching the people. We will take no part in the activities — we will simply watch the inhabitants of the town as, through the year, they go their daily rounds.

There is no better way to understand what life was like in a cliff dwelling. The ancient structures themselves do not tell the whole story, nor do the artifacts in the museum. The well-built walls and the skillfully made artifacts are ample evidence of the abilities of the people but these articles of stone, bone and wood do not tell us all we would like to know.

The real story is in the people and if we are to understand it, we must see them with our own eyes. So, after setting the scene, we will go back to Cliff Palace in the year 1268 A.D., and take our seats. And when the year has passed, we will understand what life was like in the Mesa Verde when the cliff dwellings were alive.

We shall select Cliff Palace for our experiment because it was the largest of the cliff dwellings: certainly it was the crowning achievement of the Mesa Verde people. To modern man it may seem only a village but to the Indians it was much more than that. Located almost in the center of the great mesa was the largest cave of all. In it was the greatest structure they ever built.

To the people it was the big town, the hub of their small world. In their eyes it was magnified by comparison with the hundreds of smaller cliff dwellings around it. To them it was a city, the greatest they ever knew. Certainly there could be no better place for us to see the life of those eventful days when thousands of people lived in the Mesa Verde.

Before we take up actual residence in Cliff Palace we should answer one question, a question that is asked very often. How can we know what was happening in a town that was abandoned almost seven hundred years ago? The former inhabitants have disappeared and they left no written records. How will we be able to see the intimate details in the lives of those people?

It is a good question. It is often in the minds of visitors as they walk through the silent city and listen to the stories that are told about the former inhabitants. Intimate details in the lives of the people are laid bare. Assertions are made for which there is no visible evidence. The visitor can scarcely be blamed for wearing a skeptical look in his eyes.

Our knowledge of the intimacies of the ancient life has come from a number of sources. Through intensive study, archeologists, ethnologists and historians have worked out the details that go toward making a complete story. From countless sources they have garnered the bits of information that fit together in jig-saw fashion to give us a picture of life in a cliff dwelling. Unfortunately, some pieces of the picture are still missing; here and there are rather large and distressing holes. In some lines of research, blank walls have been encountered and mystery still enshrouds some of the phases we would like most of all to see.

On the whole, though, the picture is rather complete. By fitting together all of the bits of knowledge that have been given to us by various scientists we can see very well the happenings in one of the ancient villages.

The archeologist has given us the general background of the people of Cliff Palace. Decades of research have revealed the development of the Pueblo Indians during their one thousand year occupation of the Mesa Verde. But the archeologist has gone even farther and, in a general way, has traced the people back through countless centuries to their original home in a far continent. We shall see this long story of development in later chapters.

Originally the people came from Asia, drifting into America across the Bering Sea. From Alaska they drifted south and, after endless generations, reached the Southwest. Up to this time they had lived as roving hunters but somewhere in the

Southwest they met other Indians who were farmers. This new life appealed to them and, borrowing the precious seeds, they gradually became a farming people.

At about the time of Christ they moved into the Mesa Verde region and soon some of them were living on the Mesa Verde itself. At first their culture was simple but for a thousand years it developed. Finally it reached its peak in the thirteenth century when Cliff Palace and the other cliff dwellings were built.

In addition to giving us the background, the archeologists have given us the material details of the ancient city. Through their excavations the actual remains have been brought to light, studied and interpreted. When we walk through Cliff Palace we appreciate the tremendous overhanging cave roof that protected the entire city. We see the results of the physical labors of the people; the houses with their smooth walls and bright paintings, the storage rooms, kivas, open courts, narrow winding passageways, firepits, and in the back of the cave, the trash room where the turkeys roosted.

In the nearby museum we see the actual physical remains, the skeletons and mummies, of the people themselves. We see their clothing and their jewelry. There also are the utensils and tools; pottery, basketry, bows and arrows, stone knives, bone awls and needles, grinding stones, fire drills, planting sticks, stone axes and mauls; an endless array of things that were once in common use.

All of this has been given to us by the archeologist. He has shown us the long background of the people and has unearthed, restored and interpreted the actual material things from the ruin. To many people these things seem cold and inanimate. They seem dead; just stone, bone, wood and clay. There is life in them, though, for they are the expressions of the desires, ambitions, loves and hates of the people. Every single article was produced because of some human desire or need.

The person who keeps this in mind is able to walk through Cliff Palace, even today, and see the former inhabitants, for in the results of their efforts they still live. Many visitors forget this and do not see the people. Even the archeologist often fails to see them as he is a scientist who deals only with realities. Sometimes he can not see the people for the walls.

Historians have also contributed to the story of ancient Indian life. The musty records of the early explorers of the Southwest contain many extremely valuable observations concerning the Pueblo Indians. These the historians have ferreted out.

As early as 1540, the Spaniards began to enter the Pueblo country when Coronado traversed almost the entire area. Other Spanish explorers followed Coronado. Missions were established in many of the pueblos and for three centuries the Spaniards were in close contact with the Indians. Later the American explorers entered the Southwest and they, too, came in contact with the Indians. The chronicles of these explorers, both Spanish and American, contain many passages concerning the life and customs of the Pueblo people. Many of these early records have been translated and compiled and from them we gain knowledge of Pueblo life during the last four centuries. It is true that not all of the observations were accurate. Many were spiced with prejudice and deliberate fallacy but still they have been of value.

The Spaniards came into the Southwest less than three centuries after the Pueblo Indians left the Mesa Verde and drifted to the South. The Indians were still living in terraced pueblos. They were still farmers; corn, beans and squash still dominated the food bowl out of which each family ate. In a material way they had changed little, so it is safe to assume they had changed little in their social and religious customs.

Even after the white men arrived there was little change in the life of the Pueblo Indians until within the last few decades. For that reason the early records, when properly interpreted, add much to our knowledge of the ancient cultures.

Ethnologists have done a vast amount of work that supplements the labors of the archeologist and the historian. The ethnologist is a scientist who makes an actual detailed study of a group of living Indians. Every cultural detail is recorded and there have been ethnologists who knew almost as much about the Indians whom they studied as the Indians knew about themselves.

Some of the ethnologists have lived in the pueblos for long periods of time. In some cases they have been accepted by the

Indians and have even been taken into the priesthood. An outstanding example was Mr. Frank Hamilton Cushing, an ethnologist who lived in the pueblo of Zuni from 1879 to 1884. He learned the Zuni language, was adopted into the Macaw clan and was initiated into various religious societies. He participated in the religious ceremonies, wore native costume, ate native foods and took part in the various occupations and pastimes. Before he left the pueblo he became the second chief of the tribe and was made the head priest of the Bow, one of the highest religious offices.

Such men as Cushing have given us detailed knowledge of the legends, religion, ceremonies, social customs and daily life of the modern Pueblo Indians. Since these Indians are descendants of the ancient Pueblo Indians, this knowledge has enabled us to answer many questions.

The person who walks into Cliff Palace and views a kiva for the first time has not the slightest chance of guessing its original purpose. It is absolutely remote from anything he has ever seen. But when he is told that these same strange rooms still survive in the present-day pueblos and are used as club rooms and ceremonial chambers, the use becomes immediately apparent. In the center of the ancient kiva floor is a tiny hole that has no obvious purpose. That same hole is still found in some of the present-day kivas and the Indian explains that it is the spirit entrance to the earth. Even the wisest archeologist could never have guessed that.

Without the help of present-day Indians it would be almost impossible to answer questions about such non-material things as religion and social customs. We can dig up the bones of a man, every bone he ever possessed. But who can look at those bones and tell how many wives he had? Some people think it should show but it doesn't. In order to answer the question we simply go to the descendants of that man. Without doubt they still have the same customs.

From all this it can be seen that the ethnologist has added much to our story. Since the Pueblo Indians of today are the descendants of the Pueblo Indians of a few centuries ago, a thorough knowledge of them is the soundest approach to an understanding of the ancient people.

In using our knowledge of the modern Pueblo Indians in an effort to picture life in ancient times we are faced with an important question. How much have the customs changed because of the influence of the Spaniards?

As soon as the Spaniards entered the Pueblo country they established missions in the Indian pueblos. The native religion was suppressed and a new religion was forced upon the Pueblo people. In the Rio Grande area in New Mexico this foreign pressure was strongest and there can be little doubt that the native Indian religion and customs have changed to some extent. In the western pueblos of the Zunis and Hopis the Spanish pressure was not so great. Missions were maintained at Zuni only intermittently and among the Hopis for only a short time. As a result the native Pueblo religion and customs of these western pueblos have undergone less change and they will be used, for the most part, in our effort to picture the ancient life of the Mesa Verde.

As we move into Cliff Palace to spend a year with the inhabitants we must not forget the sources of our knowledge. First, we have the cultural background of the people, their rise from roving hunters to stable agriculturists; second, we have the great ruin itself and the things the people left in it; third, we have the interpretations of Indians who are descendants of the ancient people. All these will be added together to complete the picture. We must realize, however, that there are questions still unanswered: some problems will never satisfactorily be solved. But if we use the knowledge that has been gained and remain within the realm of plausibility we shall be able to follow the people very well as they go through their daily lives.

Now we are ready to turn back the centuries. We are ready to walk into Cliff Palace and live with the people. How better can we see the life of the ancient city? We will follow the men, women and children, as they go through the daily round of life. Spring, summer, autumn and winter will pass. We will see the work, the play, the dreams, the desires, the happiness and the bitter disappointments in the lives of the people. We will take no part in the activities. We will merely watch.

What year shall it be?

Seven centuries ago Cliff Palace was a busy, happy city of about four hundred people

35

It makes no difference as long as it is a good year, a normal year, with an abundance of snow and rain. That was the most important factor because of its effect upon the harvests. Tree ring records show that 1261 and 1262 were normal years, also 1265, 1266, 1267, 1268, 1269, 1271 and 1272. All of those were good years and that was the time when Cliff Palace was at its height. The people had been living in the cave for many years and the great city was surely at its peak.

Let's take the year 1268. It is as good as any. It was a normal, happy year for the people of Cliff Palace.

Let the centuries roll back – it is 1268 A. D.

As we walk into Cliff Palace we find it at the very peak of its development. For generations it has been growing until now it fills the great sheltering cave. There are over two hundred one-room houses in the city; they fill the cave from end to end and rise in terraces to a height of three and even four stories. At the south end and again at the north end the terraced structures rise to touch the cave roof.

Scattered about the city are twenty-three kivas, the underground ceremonial chambers. Their flat roofs serve as courts where many of the activities take place. The roofs of the terraced houses are also the scene of much activity and throughout the city many ladders lean against the walls, leading from one level to the next.

To us Cliff Palace seems like a great two-hundred-room apartment house. To the occupants it is a city of two hundred houses, occupied by scores of families. Over four hundred people live in the city; they swarm about the courts and over the roofs like so many busy brown ants.

As we enter the city we notice immediately the appearance of the people. They are typical Indians. They seem rather short, the men averaging about five feet four inches in height and the women about five feet. They are heavy-set and as we watch them we get the impression that as a rule they are a short, stocky people. The skin color varies from light to dark brown; some of them are so dark they seem almost black. The eyes are also brown and the hair varies from dark brown to a deep lustrous black.

The people have broad heads and the back of each head is flattened, a deformity caused in infancy by a hard cradle board. The faces are broad and the cheek bones are prominent. Occasionally we notice "slanting" Mongoloid eyes. The people seem to have certain Mongoloid tendencies although they are not a pure Mongoloid type.

This town where we are going to spend the year is simply a large terraced apartment house built in a great cave. In the two hundred or more rooms live at least four hundred Indians, short, stocky, brown-skinned people whom we will know well before the year is over.

The centuries have rolled back to the year 1268 A.D., and we take our seats on a roof.

It is spring.

4

SPRING

Spring is a happy, joyous time for the people of Cliff Palace and there is much laughter and gaiety in the great cave. The bleak, uncomfortable winter is over; there is a feeling of freedom and broken bonds. Everything in nature indicates that a new year and new life are beginning and the people respond just as do the animals and plants.

The winter that is ending has been cold and even though the people became accustomed to it there was suffering and sadness. Many of the older people who were afflicted with rheumatism and arthritis suffered terribly and the children developed colds and other diseases against which the medicine men were powerless. Several deaths occurred in Cliff Palace last winter and there was sadness and fear in the cave city. These misfortunes were caused by witches, who are evil human beings with only one desire – to injure and destroy the people. Winter is the season when witches are most active so it is a time of fear and dread for the inhabitants of the town.

Now spring is here and the people are gay and lighthearted. Spring is ever a happy time for farmers for the miracle of new life never loses its thrill. Spring, the season of new life; summer, the season of growth and development; autumn, the season of ripening and harvest; winter, the season of suffering, death and sorrow. Then spring comes again and the eternal cycle has another joyous beginning.

In March the sun begins to be warm. During the morning, while still in the shadow, the cave is cold but in the afternoon when the sun creeps in, it is very pleasant. Some days the sun is actually hot as it beats into the sheltered cave. Chipmunks and squirrels, even the lizards, come out of hibernation to sun themselves on the warm rocks. The Indians do likewise.

As the sun begins to climb into the cave each afternoon the people come out to meet it. Uncomfortable winter clothing is thrown aside and soon most of the inhabitants of the cave are sunning themselves on the front terraces. Everyone is happy.

There is much laughter and boisterous shouting. The aged men and women bring their rheumatic bones out into the warm sunlight and immediately feel new life. Gaunt old men, whose creaking joints have not climbed the cliff trails for years, get a new gleam in their eyes as they vow they will raise a crop of corn this summer. Aged women begin to twist their gnarled fingers as they dream of making pottery again.

The able-bodied men sit in small groups, dreaming and talking of the planting time that is coming. Wrinkled old priests assure them that it will be a fine season. All signs are right; the gods are smiling on their people. The women think of new pottery they must make, repairs they plan for their houses, and marriages they must arrange for their daughters. Young wives, in whom romance has not been dulled by too many children, playfully comb the lice from their husbands' heads and dream of babies soon to come. Spring is a fine time for that.

Here and there young unmarried men lean against the walls, presumably dozing in the sun. But they are the busiest of all. Each one is endeavoring to catch the eye of some dusky young maiden whose full-rounded curves are causing her mother to think of a son-in-law. The young man's eyes seldom connect; the ever vigilant eyes of mothers and aunts come between.

The really active members of the populace are the children. Some play on the trash pile in front of the cave; others scramble over the boulders that litter the slope below. Their rich brown skins flash in the sun as they endeavor to make up in one afternoon for all of the cold inactivity of the winter. Their shouts and laughter are mingled with the barking of their dogs and the gobbling of the turkeys they are disturbing. During the winter the turkeys stayed close to the cave but now they are scattered over the slope, nipping off the early buds and searching for the first insects of spring.

Not every March day is warm: some are blustery with the changeable weather of spring. A clear blue sky turns black in only a few minutes and heavy wet snow swirls into the canyons. The snow soon changes to rain, then a cool breeze swings down from the north and the rain becomes icy pellets of sleet. In a few minutes the clouds blow away and the warm sun shines again on a dripping, steaming world. Sometimes during the night, warm, wet snow falls, snow so heavy that its weight snaps limbs

Life in a cliff dwelling. Museum diorama of Spruce Tree House

from the trees. The warm rocks and the bright sun melt it rapidly and often there is a roaring waterfall over the front of Cliff Palace cave as the water rushes off the mesa top.

The weather grows steadily warmer and winter is left behind. There is much activity in the city. Everyone is up at sunrise and the work of the day is immediately started. After several hours of work, breakfast is eaten late in the morning, then the activities are resumed. The second and last meal of the day, an early supper, brings an end to the day's activities.

During the winter the cave became damp and musty; everything needs to be aired out. Clothing, blankets, robes and floor mats are spread out on the terraces and roofs to bake in the sun. The women tie small bunches of stiff grass with cords and with these brush-like brooms sweep the houses and courtyards thoroughly. Trash is swept into the back of the cave where the turkeys roost or out on the ever-growing trash pile which slides far down the slope in front.

Even the kivas, the underground ceremonial rooms, are cleaned and the walls are replastered to hide the soot that has accumulated. The men do some of the cleaning but women are often invited to help, especially with the plastering. It is considered a great honor for a woman to be chosen to plaster a kiva.

A major part of the spring work is the repairing of houses. It is work that never seems to end for repairs and alterations are always in progress in some part of the city except in the winter when it is too cold. Spring is the best time for the repair work as there is an abundance of water for the mortar and the home owners are filled with a desire to build and improve. Cracks are merely filled with mud and small chinking stones. Sometimes a small section of wall has bulged dangerously and must be replaced. Often the walls have been built on a foundation of loose trash and as a result, settle until they are in danger of falling. Such walls, sometimes entire rooms, must be torn down and rebuilt. Sometimes a house is deserted by its owners for some reason and gradually goes to ruin. As it crumbles the stones and the roof poles are used in the repairing or building of other houses. It is an endless cycle, this building and repairing of houses, and all stages of it can be seen in the town almost any time.

Most of the repair work is done by the women for the houses belong to them. When there is heavy work, new poles to cut or new stones to shape, the men help but even then the women supervise.

Very often, as is true among all people, the women change the decorations of their houses. A new whim stirs the house-wife's imagination and in an hour's time the entire scheme is changed. The husband never knows what to expect when he re-turns from a day in the fields. Decorations are easily applied for they consist of thin layers of clay mud, spread on the walls with the hands. Sometimes the entire house is smoothly plas-tered with red, yellow, grey, brown or white clay. Other houses are plastered only on the outside; some only on the inside. Here is a house that is plastered half-way down from the ceil-ing; next door is one that is plastered half-way up from the floor.

Many of the walls are decorated with bright paintings. Red ochre makes a rich red plaster, while up on the mesa top is a layer of clay that gives a clean chalky-white color. When the two are combined, the effect is striking. Most of the paintings are small; the picture of an animal, a geometric design or perhaps just a band of color across a wall. In the center of Cliff Palace is a house that has a row of nine, bright red hands painted above the door. The woman who lives there placed her left hand on the wall and traced it nine times. Then she filled in the outlines with red ochre to produce the odd decoration.

Near the south end of the town is the most beautifully deco-rated house of all. It is the third-floor room of the great four-story tower, the tallest structure in the cave. The young lady who lives there is very artistic and all four inside walls are beautifully painted in red and white. The lower half of the walls she painted with red ochre. The upper half she covered with the chalky-white clay. Where the two bands of color came to-gether she painted large red triangles in groups of three. Thus the edge of the red border consists of three triangles, or peaks, then a straight line, three more triangles, and so on around the room. On the white upper portions of the walls are geometric designs painted in red; parallel straight lines, parallel zigzag lines and parallel fringed lines.

The painting was cleverly done and the final effect is strikingly beautiful. The young woman is artistic in everything she does. Her pottery designs are the best in the city and she even wears her little yucca-string skirt at an artistically rakish angle. The men of the neighborhood often speak of her artistry. Their wives speak of her extremely poor cooking.

As spring progresses the weather grows warmer. The wet, heavy snows come less frequently and most of the days are full of sunshine. Sometimes sharp winds sweep off the snow-covered mountains to the north and cut across the mesa tops but the sheltering cave keeps them out of Cliff Palace.

As April arrives the effects of sunshine and moisture become evident. The grass is green, leaves are coming out on the shrubs and the earth is broken by the first tender shoots of myriads of growing plants. There is a damp, earthy smell in the canyons; the dank odor of rotting leaf mold, the heavy odor of wet clay. Through it all is the delicate fragrance of growing, budding plants. Back from the south come the first birds and spring is definitely in the Mesa Verde.

The earth-loving Indians are bursting with restless energy and everyone is busy. Sometimes the town is almost deserted as the call of spring draws them out of the cave. The cliffs echo with the laughter of small children as they play along the slopes and down in the bottom of the canyon. During the winter in the shadowy cave their skins became pale but already the spring sun is tanning them to a warm brown. Their hearts are light; they are like unrestrained little brown animals as they play the days away. They have fewer cares and troubles than the chipmunks and squirrels whose lives they make miserable. Each small boy carries a bow and each one knows how to set cord snares in the runways among the rocks. Sometimes a small hunter is successful and the cliffs ring with his exultant shouts as he brings a chipmunk or a squirrel or even a fat rat to his mother. At the next meal he is a hero and receives the choicest morsels from his kill.

Some of the older boys go out on the mesas for larger game. The wet, silent earth makes it easy for them to stalk the deer and mountain sheep that have never been alarmed by the thundering reports of firearms. At long range their flint-tipped arrows are not effective but they are clever stalkers and at close range the silent arrows are deadly. In the evening they return with their game. They trot proudly down the precipitous trails and through the city, hoping that the eyes of the maidens will rest upon them. But the soft brown eyes are always turned away – still they see.

Most of the men climb up to the mesa-top fields even though they are too wet to be worked. Their love of the soil draws them to their farms and they boast about the crops they intend to grow, or listen to the old men as they tell of the miraculous crops of bygone years.

Even though it is too early to farm, the men are soon busy. New land must be cleared to replace fields that have been farmed too long. The sagebrush and shrubs are pulled up or are dug out of the ground with digging sticks. Small trees are cut with stone axes but the larger trees are burned and in all parts of the Mesa Verde columns of smoke rise as men of the different villages clear the land. Usually this clearing of new land is done in the late winter and early spring when the cool damp weather makes it easier for the men to control the fires. If the burning were done in the summer, forest fires would result and vast areas would be rendered uninhabitable through loss of fire wood and logs for house construction.

The fields are owned in common by the village but they are alloted to the clans, which are groups of families related through the female line. The clan in turn allots the fields to its various households, or families. After a generation or two the lands farmed by members of a household seem almost to belong to it but the real control is by the clan. As long as a piece of land is farmed properly it remains with the household but if it is neglected or if the household dies out, the clan heads allot it to other households within the clan. Since the clans are matrilineal, with descent of property in the female line, a man farms land belonging to his wife's clan.

In the early spring no one is busier than the women. Each day they scour the canyons and mesas for early plants that will lend variety to the diet. During the late winter the food became monotonous. Day after day it was cornbread, beans and meat. Principally it was cornbread and although it was prepared in a number of ways it became tiresome.

The early spring plants bring a welcome variation to this restricted diet. The green shoots of beeweed and tansy mustard and the first tender leaves of saltbush make delicious greens when boiled with pieces of fat and a dash of salt. Wild onions and juniper berries add an exciting flavor to a pot of deer meat stew. The puff-ball, a spherical, fungus-like growth six or eight inches in diameter, is sought eagerly after each warm spring rain. Toasted slices of puff-ball, eaten with a sauce made of salt and wild onions, are a real spring delicacy. Innumerable plants are edible and by countless generations of experimenting the Indian women have discovered their good qualities. They know exactly how to use each plant and new aromas rise from the cooking pots.

During the winter the people ate the monotonous food because they needed the nourishment. Now they eat for the joy of eating. Eyes gleam with anticipation as each family gathers around the fire in the late afternoon while the mother prepares the main meal of the day. There is cornbread, made in any one of a dozen ways. Deer meat is being roasted or boiled, or is bubbling in a thick stew. A pot of greens is stewing or a pot of beans, flavored with some spring plant, boils on the fire. A great pot of thin corn gruel, which will be drunk as a tea, simmers on its bed of coals. At last the food is ready and the steaming pots are placed on the ground in the midst of the family group.

As soon as all is ready the man of the family selects a sample of food from each pot; a few beans, a pinch of greens, a small piece of meat, a bit of bread, a few drops of tea. These he throws into the fire as an offering to the gods. Then the eating begins.

The only tools are the fingers and they are plunged eagerly into the food, hot though it may be. Chunks of meat are picked out and if too hot are held on a piece of bread. Bones are gnawed on, then dropped back into the pot as the fingers are needed for something else. Dunking is common and the bread is used to scoop up the thick stew. Toothless old men, becoming impatient, pick up the bowls and drink over the edge. There are long-handled ladles for dipping out the soup and broth, and stein-like mugs for the tea.

During the meal there is little talking; the accent is on the food. The only noise is the licking of fingers and the loud smacking of lips that express appreciation for especially succulent morsels. As the men settle back, swollen from over-eating, they seek relief in deep rumbling belches, each of which is a pat on the back for the cook. No words are necessary for a slow rumbling belch is far more expressive. It speaks of a full, happy stomach, complete relaxation and sleepy content-ment. Each belch brings happiness to the fond wife and mother and she smiles as she removes the empty pots from the midst of her gorged and sleepy family.

Darkness is still an hour away but as the sun drops behind the opposite canyon rim the chill of the spring evening creeps into the cave. Women sit by the fires, robes around their shoulders, and visit idly. The men and older boys go to their kivas to talk, to doze, or perhaps to gamble a little. The chil-dren, following the shouted directions of their mothers, gather the turkeys which have been feeding on the trash pile in front of the town and drive them into the rear of the cave where they will be safe from prowling night animals.

As darkness falls the day's activities are ended and quiet settles over the city. Mats, skins and blankets are rolled out on the floors of the houses and soon the people of Cliff Palace are asleep. The quiet of the night is broken only by the snoring of tired men and the barking of a fox across the canyon. The tiny sliver of a new moon sinks behind the western mesa leav-ing brilliant, low-hung stars to watch over the sleeping people.

During the early spring one of the most important activities of the women is the making of new pottery. Very little was made during the winter because of the cold but much was broken. Numb fingers often let the vessels slip and now each woman needs to replenish her stock of water jars, cooking pots, bowls, ladles and mugs. The greatest need is for the large water jars. In the early summer there will be a long period of dry weather. For at least a month, possibly for two months, there may not be a drop of rain on the Mesa Verde. The springs will dwindle and the great pools in the bottom of the canyon will shrink. There must be additional stored water.

There are no wells or cisterns so water will be stored in the large jars. The women must make many of them, each one large enough to hold several gallons of water. During the late spring rains they will be filled and set away in small storage rooms that were emptied of their corn and beans during the winter. When the dry weather comes the stored water will be of vital importance.

The women of Cliff Palace make the beautiful black-on-white pottery that is typical of all the people of the Mesa Verde. They are proud of the graceful shapes and exact designs and each woman strives to excel her neighbors. All of the women use the same methods and there is a surprising sameness about their products. Each one varies her designs and no two pieces are exactly alike but all are of a standardized type. Each piece proclaims its Mesa Verde origin.

The women are very proud of their pottery and seldom swerve from the conventional type. Sometimes when the men go to distant regions on trading trips they bring home a few pieces of foreign pottery. Their wives compare this pottery with their own and are always satisfied. They feel that their wares excel all others and continue to make the same types their mothers and grandmothers made.

Pottery making is a long, detailed process requiring much skill and only after many years of practice are women able to make pieces of the finest quality. Each step must be carefully and thoroughly executed or the final result will not make a woman's husband proud when he compares her pottery with that of the other women.

Two ingredients are needed for the actual construction; pottery clay and a tempering material. The clay occurs in a shale layer at the foot of the upper cliff of the canyon wall. There are many deposits, large and small, and each woman has a favorite place from which she obtains her clay. Up the canyon from Cliff Palace, at the head of the right-hand fork, is an excellent deposit that is favored by many of the women.

The nights are now without freezing temperatures that would render the digging too difficult so the women begin to make pottery. Early in the morning the potter leaves Cliff Palace and sets out for her favorite clay bed. She carries a large basket and a digging stick and is accompanied by any of her daughters who are learning the art. The clay is usually soft and easy to dig and she soon returns with a basket of blue-gray earth.

The clay is spread out in the sun to dry and all stones and foreign particles are picked out. After drying thoroughly it is ground very fine on a metate, the same flat stone on which corn is ground. It is now ready for use.

The tempering material comes from an odd source. The woman simply goes out on the trash pile below the cave and picks up a quantity of broken pottery. This she grinds up just as she did the clay until it looks like fine sand. This tempering material is very important for it keeps the vessels from shrinking and cracking as they dry. Many centuries ago the ancestors of these women used sand and grit for temper. Some still use them but most of the women use ground-up potsherds. They are just as good and are much easier to obtain. Year after year the broken pots have been ground up and used again. Some of the particles the women are using today may have been used by their ancestors centuries ago.

When the clay and the temper are ready they are mixed, about one part of temper being used to two parts of clay. With her fingers the potter mixes the dry materials very thoroughly for a poor mix will give the pottery an uneven quality. Finally she is satisfied and water is added until she has a thick, heavy paste that does not stick to her hands as she works it. After this paste has been very thoroughly kneaded, actual construction of the pot begins.

From the mass of paste the potter pinches a small piece. With the palm of her hand she rolls it on a smooth stone until she has a rope of clay smaller in diameter than her little finger and several inches in length. The paste is so strong that she can pick the roll up without breaking it. Starting at one end she begins to coil this rope of clay around and around on itself, just as a snail shell is coiled. As she adds each coil she pinches it to the last one with her thumb and forefinger. When the rope of clay is completely coiled she rolls out another and adds it to the first. Coil after coil she adds until the rough pot is completed. At this point it is merely a long slender rope of clay which has been coiled around and around, up and up, into the desired shape, each coil being carefully pinched to the one below. The spiral nature is very evident and hundreds of evenly spaced thumbprints remain as evidence of the pinching together of coils.

Black-on-white pottery
Ladle, double mug, mug and bowls

If a cooking vessel is desired the inside of the jar is smoothed carefully but the outside is left rough and corrugated. Nothing is to be gained by smoothing and decorating the outside of a cooking jar for it will soon be blackened with soot.

If a water jar, or a bowl is being made, the work is only half done for it must be smoothed and decorated. Very carefully the potter rubs the vessel until the inside and outside are as smooth as she can make them. The vessel is still pliable and by working with her hands and a curved piece of gourd rind she can correct the shape slightly to make up for any mistakes she made in the coiling. At last the vessel is smooth and shapely and the potter is satisfied. She places it in the sun to dry and begins to coil another.

After a number of vessels have dried thoroughly in the sun the next step begins. From the mesa top, where it occurs just under the red top soil, the potter has brought a quantity of white clay. A small amount of this is ground up and mixed with water until a white, soupy liquid results. This is the "slip" and it is painted over the entire surface of the vessels giving them a chalky, white covering. Before the slip has dried, each pot is carefully polished with a smooth pebble. Short, brisk strokes are used and the entire surface is polished until it shines. This polishing is a tedious but important step for the smoothness, luster and hardness of the finished vessel depend upon it.

At last the pots are ready for the decorations and this is the part the potter likes best of all. It is her opportunity to demonstrate her creative ability. On Mesa Verde pottery the designs are always black, a color that is made from a local plant. Tender shoots of the common beeweed are boiled until a thick, brown liquid results. Pottery designs are painted with this liquid.

Out of thin air the woman snatches a design. She has a fierce pride in her ability to create these designs for she knows that later her finished pots will have to bear comparison with those of her neighbors. No tracings or trial pictures are made. She merely selects one of the sun-dried vessels, notes its size and shape and develops in her mind a design that will fit it. Following this mental picture she paints the vessel with the brown liquid. The brush is a small piece of yucca leaf, one end of which has been chewed to loosen the fibers. Her free-hand strokes are swift and sure and soon the vessel bears an accurate, carefully-balanced geometric design. At this stage it is drab looking for the brown lines are not attractive.

At last, after many hours of tiresome work, the potter has a number of pots ready for firing. This is the crucial step and the excellence of the pottery depends upon its success. The pots are carried down to one of the lower terraces at the front of the cave and stacked in a shallow pit that has been scooped out. Over them the potter piles the fuel; wood, bark and cakes of rotting humus from under the trees. When it is ignited it burns and smoulders, subjecting the pots to an intense heat.

When she is satisfied that the pottery is well-fired, she rakes it out of the fire, polishes it with a piece of cloth or buckskin and her work is finished. The brown paint has been changed by the heat to a deep black that stands out in striking contrast against the light gray background. From the simple ingredients; clay, ground potsherds and beeweed, has come this beautiful, enduring pottery. It is the highest artistic expression of the Mesa Verde people.

As the potter finishes her work she places the finest pieces in a row along the edge of the terrace or on her roof for all of the women to see. The poorer pieces she puts back in the dark corners of the house where they will not be noticed. Out of the corner of her eyes she sees other women placing their pottery on display and she smiles with satisfaction as she notes that her work is as fine as any. There is much good-natured competition among the women and each one tries to out-do her neighbors.

As the spring progresses tremendous quantities of pottery are made. All through the cave women are at work and pottery in all stages of construction is to be seen along all of the terraces and in every courtyard. Spring is the most popular time for this task. The winter is too cold; in the summer water is often scarce. During the spring all conditions are perfect and the nimble fingers are busy until every household is equipped with an ample supply of vessels of all kinds.

Occasionally, during the spring, a marriage takes place in Cliff Palace. When this happens there is much excitement and

Black-on-white jars and corrugated jar on yucca fiber jar rest

activity among the two clans affected. The clans are social divisions within the tribe. Each individual is born into a clan and that remains his social group throughout his life. In Cliff Palace, with its large population, there are many clans while in a small village there may be only one or two. The clans have very little to do with the religious life; they are a part of the social organization.

The pueblo society is matrilineal which merely means that the line of descent is through the women, not through the men. A child is born into its mother's clan, never into its father's. Property also belongs to the women and inheritance is figured through the female line. The husband lives with his wife in her house and his children belong to her clan. Marriage can never take place between two members of the same clan. This is a rigidly enforced taboo and the boy and girl must belong to different social groups. All of the members of a clan are considered as brothers and sisters, consequently there is little temptation to overstep this rule.

When a boy reaches the age of seventeen or eighteen and seems to be growing into manhood, his family begins to think of marriage for him. It is the responsibility of his elders to arrange this for there can be little happiness for a single person in a society of this type.

The boy himself has little opportunity for active romance. For some time he has been sending highly expressive glances in the direction of a certain young lady of a neighboring clan, glances loaded with question marks, flattery and many other signs from that most universal of all signal codes. Now and then an answering message flashes from her warm, brown eyes. In a very short while, and without a spoken word, an understanding grows up between them. Each would like to slip away to some quiet nook in the cliffs to take the matter up somewhat more directly but it is virtually impossible and decidedly unwise. The girl's mother and her aunts have not missed a single one of those expressive glances. They do not disapprove in the slightest but they never give the girl a chance to slip away into the twilight. They may not distrust the girl but they certainly do not trust the spring moon that bathes the canyons in its warm, yellow light. Sometimes a young couple, unable to resist the call, does slip away into the night but it is very foolish.

There is no secrecy in this crowded community and a twilight tryst never goes unnoticed. The juicy morsel spreads for Cliff Palace, being full of human beings, has its gossips. The marriage value of the young lady is lowered.

In the normal course of events the young man who has been carrying on the optical conversation with the young lady is finally unable to curb his emotions. He goes to his favorite uncle, or possibly to his mother and pours out his heart. Boasting of his manhood and his hunting and farming abilities he concludes that it is high time for him to have a home of his own. And he would like to marry a certain young lady.

Immediately a family council is called and the proposition is discussed at length. If the elders do not approve of the young lady, the young man is immediately squelched. There is no resisting the decision. The brokenhearted youngster will either nurse his sorrow until another maiden captures his fancy or meekly marry some girl whom his family selects.

Marriage is an important function and the union of strong healthy boys and girls is a responsibility that falls on the older clan members. Occasionally a headstrong youth who has allowed a deep, long-distance love to grow upon him rebels against a dictated marriage. In his heart, however, is an inborn, confident reverence for his elders and he is soon frowned into line.

If, on the other hand, the family council approves of his judgment, a delegation is soon sent to talk with the family of the girl. The virtues of the boy are extolled at great length and there is a mention of certain presents that the boy's family will give to the family of the girl. The relatives of the girl tell of her virtue, industry and excellent health and let it be known that certain presents will be expected.

If the two families fail to reach an agreement the romance of the young couple is ended, but if they finally talk around to happy settlement, the next step is up to the young lady. Shortly after sunrise the next morning she goes to the boy's house and for four days grinds corn in front of the boy's mother to prove that she can do this most important work. It is a backbreaking task but she keeps at it diligently, knowing that her work must be satisfactory. At the end of the four-day period, the boy's relatives examine the results of her labor. If the amount of corn meal does not please them the marriage is called off and the heartbroken young lady returns to her house.

If, however, they are satisfied with her grinding the marriage is agreed upon. It will not take place for weeks but there is much to be done. The boy and his family must get the gifts ready and it is the custom for the girl and her relatives to build a house.

In addition to presents which his family has promised to give to the girl's family, the boy makes certain personal presents for his bride-to-be. He may make her a fine pair of sandals and may weave her a soft, warm feather blanket or even a beautiful white blanket of cotton.

The weaving of a cotton blanket may send him far afield. If his near relatives do not happen to have enough cotton on hand, he is forced to make a long journey to the south. The Mesa Verde people do not raise cotton and it is obtained by trade with tribes in the warmer lowlands. There are several men in Cliff Palace and other nearby cliff dwellings who are in need of cotton so an expedition is formed. These journeys are made each year and many of the older men are familiar with the route. Some of them act as guides for the young fellows who are going for the first time.

The Mesa Verde lacks certain important things; salt, seashells, cotton, turquoise and obsidian. In order to get these articles the men trade with other Indians who live to the south. Most of the men make occasional trading trips but some are professional traders who spend much of their time on long trading journeys.

For salt they must go to a salt lake 200 miles to the south. The salt is gathered around the edge of the lake, either by the men themselves or by other people with whom they trade. If the salt is dry it is carried home in bags but if it is gathered while wet, it is patted into balls which, when dried, are hard as rocks.

Obsidian and turquoise are obtained far to the southeast, near the big river. It is a journey of 200 miles to the turquoise mine but the deep blue stones are the finest known and are well worth the trip. Another source of turquoise is only 150 miles to the east, across the high mountains, but the Mesa Verde men seldom go in that direction. Hostile Indians live in the mountains and the parties do not always return.

Sea shells come from the great ocean far to the southwest but the men do not go all the way to the ocean for them. The shells are traded from tribe to tribe as they move inland. By the time the Mesa Verde men get them from Pueblo Indians who live to the southwest, the price is very high.

Cotton, which will not grow in the Mesa Verde because of the cool nights, must be obtained from other Pueblo Indians who live to the south and southwest. It grows well in the warmer lowlands and is one of the most important trade items. The men trade for the raw cotton fibers, usually, and weave them into blankets after they return home.

Trading expeditions are happy experiences for the men. They not only love to travel and meet other people but they love to trade. All along the route are villages of friendly Pueblo Indians and the travelers are honored guests in these villages. Traders are always welcome for they not only offer an opportunity for trading but they bring news from far countries.

The departure of the trading party is a gala occasion and all the people in Cliff Palace join to give it a noisy send-off. It is the first expedition of the spring so a great many men are in the party. As they start down the canyon, each man carries a large pack on his back. Most of a man's burden consists of the things he will offer in trade when he reaches his destination. Perhaps he has tanned buckskin: the soft white leather has great value in the lands to the south where deer are scarce. He may have the skin of a spotted fawn he choked to death last summer. For ceremonial use the skins must not be pierced by arrows so the animals are caught and choked and such skins are excellent for trading purposes. Also, he may carry a number of large, highly-polished skinning blades made from a banded stone found near the Mesa Verde. This stone is well known over the pueblo region and the blades are highly prized.

In addition to his trading materials, a man carries his bow and arrows, a blanket, a small bowl and a little food. He will be able to kill rabbits, squirrels and rats along the way and almost every night he will stop at a friendly village so little food need be carried. A small amount of parched corn, some dried meat and perhaps a little corn meal of a special type is all he will need. The corn meal was prepared last fall for this very purpose. At harvest time the fresh corn was roasted, then ground into meal. This meal was thoroughly toasted and again was ground, this time very fine. The meal is so well cooked that a man need only stir it into a bowl of cold water to have a nourishing drink. The men know all of the streams and springs along the way so there will be no hardships unless they meet enemy people.

In two weeks the men begin to return and at the end of the month all are accounted for except a small party which went to the southeast for turquoise and obsidian. They are long over-due and at last the people give them up for lost. It merely means that they encountered a band of nomadic, warlike Indians and perished. Groups of savage hunters sometimes slip into the Pueblo country to prey upon the peaceful farmers and the pressure from these nomadic Indians is being felt more and more. There was a time, many generations ago, when the Mesa Verde people had no outside enemies and their villages were scattered over a vast area. At that time they lived in open pueblos out on the mesa tops and in all the broad valleys. Then nomadic hunting Indians began to drift into the Pueblo country. They raided the small villages, murdered the men, enslaved the women and children and destroyed the crops. In the border regions which were sparsely populated, village after village was destroyed by the raiders. As the pressure increased, the farming people deserted the valleys and the open mesa tops and for the last few generations they have lived in the cliff dwellings which they built in the caves of the Mesa Verde.

Cliff Palace has not yet been molested. It is in the midst of a large group of cliff dwellings and the population is so great the enemy people have not dared attack. But the men who have returned from their trading journeys have brought news of in-creasing enemy trouble in the surrounding regions and the people know the threat is coming closer.

This spring only the one party of traders was lost to the enemy. All the others have returned to the safety of their cave home and they tell of their journeys in great detail. They were received hospitably in Pueblo villages along the way and have brought home a good supply of the things the Mesa Verde does not provide; salt, turquoise, cotton and sea shells. They have also brought news from all the country to the south. Fires burn far into the night as the people listen to the tales from the outer world. The young men who made their first trip have become heroes and they make the most of the opportunity as they tell magnificent tales of the things they have done and seen. Most of them did well with their trading but a few gambled and lost, and have returned with nothing but their loincloths. That is not serious, however, and the great cave rings with laughter as the people torment the unfortunate gamblers.

The young man who needed cotton for his marriage blanket sets up a loom in his kiva and begins to weave. Older men in the clan help him with the spinning and the blanket grows steadily. The yarn is spun by hand until it is fine and even and the young weaver listens attentively to the advice of the older men as his weaving proceeds. This blanket is an expression of his feelings for the young lady and he makes it as nearly perfect as possible.

The bride-to-be is also busy for she and her relatives on her mother's side must provide a house. The spot is chosen, either beside her mother's house or on top of it and the walls begin to rise. The house will be the property of the girl and her wishes are respected but the real supervisor of operations is her mother. She is experienced in such matters and her tongue is sharp as she directs the many workers. All of the girl's clan relatives help. The men do the heavy work of cutting roof poles and shaping the stones while the mortar work and plastering is the work of the women.

Stones for the house are not quarried. The men simply go out along the canyon slopes and pick up small rocks which are of the proper size, though of irregular shapes. As soon as a large pile is accumulated they begin to dress the stones. A few, well-directed blows from a heavy maul or hammer give a stone the general shape desired, then a thorough dressing with small pecking and rubbing stones gives it the final finish. The sandstone is soft and the men are skillful, so in spite of the simple tools the building stones are turned out surprisingly fast.

Mortar for the walls is prepared by the women. Gray clay is generally used and it needs only the addition of water to make a heavy, sticky mortar. The women do much of the work but they often call on the men for help. As the walls rise, prayer sticks are buried in the corners. These small, carved sticks are offerings to the Gods and assure the stability of the house. When the walls are as high as the builders' heads, three or four heavy poles are laid across as main roof supports. Over these is spread a thatch of brush and withes and the roof is finished off with a layer of adobe three or four inches thick.

It takes only a few days to build the house if the builders are in a hurry but they seldom are. The house can be completed long before the boy's weaving is finished, so the work is done leisurely. House building is a pleasant task. All of the close relatives in the girl's clan work together and the hours are filled with laughter and practical jokes. There is much feasting and, of course, a happy celebration when the house is finished.

As the little structure rises there is a deep satisfaction in the hearts of the builders. They are helping a young couple reach their ultimate goal. To the home-loving people this goal is marriage, a home and children. Their lives point toward that end.

This tiny room will be home to the young couple for the rest of their lives. It is small, not over six by eight feet in size and the roof is so low that the husband will have to duck his head to miss the beams. The one door is very small, measuring only sixteen inches in width and twenty-four inches in height. The door sill is almost three feet above the floor and it will be awkward for the short, chubby little bride who is scarcely five feet tall. She will have difficulty straddling through the high opening, and will not dare grow too fat in later years. Older women often get so heavy that they can hardly squeeze through the tiny doors. But it has always been the custom to make the doors small and time-honored custom means more than the comfort of fat women.

There are no windows in the house and it has no firepit. Few of the women have fires inside their houses and cooking is done in the courts. Some of the older women who suffer from rheumatism and arthritis have fires in their houses but the smoke is very bad.

The final step in the construction of the house is the plastering. This is left to the young bride-to-be and she does it with loving care. A smooth coat of plaster, a few red designs and the house is finished. Her husband will come to live in it with her but it will always be her property. She is terribly proud of it. Being uncivilized she feels that her home and children will be the most important things in her life.

All of the houses in Cliff Palace are much like this one. They are small, simple rooms that serve principally as sleeping quarters and for the storage of possessions. Most of the activities take place in the open courts and on the roofs of the terraced structures so there is no need for large houses. They would be difficult to warm in winter and would reduce the number of families that could live in the cave.

After weeks, sometimes months, of leisurely preparation it is time for the boy to move to the girl's house. He has finished the presents he will give to her, the house has been built and the two families have exchanged the presents originally agreed upon. There is no actual wedding ceremony. The boy moves his personal property; his clothing, weapons and tools from his mother's house to the girl's house. They are now husband and wife. Although he is only eighteen and she only fifteen they have entered the serious phase of life and must bear their share of the community responsibility.

The first few weeks of married life are difficult for the young husband. He is living in the midst of his wife's relatives who are watching him critically. If he fails to fit in, his life will not be pleasant and the marriage may not last. Most marriages, however, are successful for the young husbands, being still pliable, are able to adjust themselves to their in-laws. In some cases the house is not built until the young husband has lived for a time with the wife's relatives and is fully approved by them.

If the marriage is not a success, divorce is simple. Perhaps the husband decides it is hopeless, not because he does not love his wife, but because he can not stand her relatives. He simply picks up his personal belongings and goes back to his mother's house. If the wife decides to call it off, it is equally direct. One day when he is out hunting or working in the fields she throws all of his personal possessions out of her house. When the husband returns, he cannot argue for all of her relatives are there to defend her decision. So back to his mother he goes.

If there are children in the family they remain with the mother for children always belong to the mother's clan. They will be cared for by her relatives until she marries again.

In April a period of frenzied activity begins for the men of Cliff Palace. It will soon be planting time and the fields must be prepared for that all-important time when the precious seeds will be placed in the earth. The frost has left the soil and it is dry enough to be worked so each morning the men and boys trot up the trails to the mesa tops to spend the day preparing the soil for planting. The fields are scattered far and wide over the mesas. Most of the men from Cliff Palace have their farms nearby but some trot miles across the flat mesa tops to farm certain favored plots. These men who have descended from a thousand years of farmers have an uncanny ability to select the best areas for farming.

The fields are seldom large and they are never regular in shape. An acre here, a few acres there, they dot the mesa tops, the rich red soil standing out sharply against the green cover of the vast "green table." The heavy snows of winter have filled the earth with moisture which will carry the crops through the dry, hot weather of early summer. Then the late summer rains will come and the worries of the farmers will be over.

Many of the men like to farm in the low draws above the heads of the canyons. There is deep, rich soil there and a con- centration of moisture that produces the finest crops. Such draws are not large but they make excellent farming areas. The men even enlarge them by building terraces where the draws are too narrow and steep for normal farming. Low dams of stones are built across the drainage, seldom more than three or four feet high and twenty or thirty feet long. The heavy rains of sum- mer wash rich soil from the mesas and deposit it behind the dams. Soon each one becomes a terrace large enough for a few hills of corn, beans or squash. Sometimes there are as many as a hun- dred of these terraces in a single small draw. In a dry year, when the plants on the mesa tops die from lack of moisture, these terraces usually produce a crop. Even a slight rain causes water to drain down across them and they assure a small harvest.

The early spring work consists of clearing the trash and weeds out of the fields and stirring up the soil for planting. Dead weeds are pulled out of the ground and burned and the first green weeds of spring are prodded out of the soil with digging sticks. Some of the men even begin to stir up the soil where they will later place the seeds. Corn is sometimes planted almost a foot in the earth so each hill requires a great deal of effort. The plants grow better if the soil is loosened up so the men select the spots for the hills and begin to dig up the soil and turn it over.

The only tool is a digging stick, a slender hardwood limb that has one end sharpened into a chisel-like blade. Small digging sticks may be only an inch in diameter and a foot in length but the large ones are sometimes three inches in diameter and five feet long. The upper end of the large ones is rounded into a knob that serves as a handhold and near the base may be a prong so the foot can be used in forcing the blade into the soil.

Sometimes a stone blade is attached to the digging stick. The stone for these blades is found down across the big river, forty miles to the southwest. That is a short easy journey: the young men make the round trip in three or four days and return with long slabs of stone. For days the men grind these on pieces of sandstone until a long thin blade, two or three inches wide and from six to ten inches in length, is formed. The stone is a light tan color, with thin bands of red and brown and it takes a beautiful polish. When one of these blades is bound firmly to a long handle it makes a very serviceable tool for turning up the soil and chopping out weeds.

While the men are preparing the fields the medicine men are watching the weather very carefully. It is their duty to set the planting date. There are countless signs they must take into consideration. The return of certain birds from the south is observed and the appearance and growth of spring plants is watched carefully. The clouds and the sky are observed constantly and the wind is tested many times a day. All of these things have a meaning. Countless generations of medicine men have developed a "weather sense" and barring occasional mistakes they are quite accurate in their predictions.

The planting date finally will be set by the Sun Watcher, a priest who throughout the year observes the movements of the

Top. Old men sit in the sun and talk of better times
Bottom. A busy afternoon in a cliff dwelling

sun. Each evening, as planting time approaches, he stands on the roof of his house and notes where the setting sun sinks behind the western horizon. Each day it comes closer to a large crack in the opposite canyon wall: when it reaches the crack it will be planting time. The moon also is watched and the priests note with satisfaction that a thin new moon is climbing higher in the western sky each evening. Planting must be done while the moon is growing larger. The corn will then grow as the moon grows. If it is planted while the moon is waning the corn will wither and die.

In addition to setting the planting date, the priests must also perform certain ceremonies over the seeds that are to be planted. Spring is not an important ceremonial season for the men are too busy to spare time for the long, elaborate ceremonies. Certain rites must be performed, however, and offerings must be made to certain gods so they will smile upon the people. It is a simple form of "crop insurance."

The fertility rites are especially important for unless the gods of fertility and reproduction are pleased, the seeds will rot in the ground without sprouting. Around the precious seeds the priests and their helpers perform the ancient rites. Year after year the ritual is the same; countless generations of priests have developed this elaborate formula that is followed in the finest detail. There is endless chanting, parts of the legends are dramatized, and there are offerings of prayer sticks, corn pollen, cornmeal and perfect ears of corn. If the ceremonies are properly performed the germ gods will be pleased and the seeds will sprout and grow well.

As the end of spring draws near everything is in readiness. The germination ceremonies are over and the fields are ready for the planting. The eager farmers await the nod of the priests which will send them scurring to the fields to plunge the seeds into the earth.

In any normal year in the Mesa Verde there are several days of rain about the middle of May. The farmers like to plant their crops just before the rains come in order that they may get the greatest benefit from the moisture. If the planting is done too early, however, there is danger of late frosts so the medicine men are in a dangerous position. If they sanction the planting too soon, frosts may nip the tender young shoots, while if they hold off too long the rains may come. Not only will the planting be delayed many days but much of the benefit of the moisture will be lost.

Carefully, the priests watch the signs. The birds, the plants, the sun, the moon; everything goes through the regular progression of spring. The sun is moving farther and farther to the north and each evening the eyes of the people are on the Sun Watcher as he makes his sunset observations. At last the important day comes. As the sun sinks behind the horizon the Sun Watcher climbs down from his house top and hurries to the home of the Crier Chief. Immediately the Crier Chief steps out on his roof to make the announcement. The sun, he tells the waiting people, has reached the proper point; today it set directly behind the crack in the opposite canyon wall. It is planting time.

The next morning each man is off to his field at sunrise, carrying the various items of equipment he will need. The seed corn, only a small amount of which will be needed this first day, is carried in a pouch made from the entire skin of a fawn. The head and legs dangle grotesquely as the farmer throws the pouch over his shoulder. At harvest time last fall the finest ears of corn were selected for seed and ceremonies were performed to assure germination and growth. During the winter it was stored where it would be safe from dampness, mice and weavils.

In addition to his pouch of corn the farmer carries his planting stick, a plumed prayer stick and a small bag of corn meal. As he leaves his house, bowls of water are poured over him by the women of his household. This is symbolic of rain and will cause the summer rains to fall upon the crops.

Upon reaching his field the farmer goes to a well-known spot at the very center. With his digging stick he digs four holes, each one almost a foot deep. The first hole is north of the center spot, the second is to the west, the third is to the south and the fourth is to the east. On the west side of the northern hole he digs another which represents the sky regions and on the east side of the southern hole another which represents the lower regions.

In the center of the space bounded by the six holes he kneels, facing the east and with cornmeal paints a cross on the ground. Murmuring a prayer, he plants the plumed prayer stick in the center of the cross and sprinkles it with cornmeal.

Now he moves out of the central space and opens his bag of seed corn. Carefully he selects four grains of each color — yellow, blue, red, white, speckled and black. Returning to the central space, he kneels facing the northern hole and begins to chant. At the proper point in the chant he drops the four yellow grains into the hole. Shifting to the westward, he continues his chant and drops the four blue grains into the western hole. Chanting without a break, he goes from one hole to the next. The red corn is dropped into the southern hole, the white corn into the eastern hole, the speckled corn into the hole representing the sky regions and the black corn into the hole representing the lower regions.

Now the ceremony is over and he fills in the holes where the seeds have been planted. Picking up his pouch of seed corn and his planting stick, he plants four long rows of corn, each one starting at his little central plot. One row extends to the north, another to the west, another to the south and the final row to the east.

When his seed is exhausted, he is through for the day and returns to the village. The rest of the field can not be planted until four days have passed. During that time he will go through many rituals of prayer, will place offerings at shrines and will not eat forbidden foods. Also, he will avoid trading, gambling and certain other pleasures.

After four days have passed, the remaining portions of each field are planted. This is done without ceremony and as hurriedly as possible for everything indicates that the May rains are near. There is a light haze in the sky and the air feels warm and damp. The moisture is in the air; only an east wind is needed to bring it down. Planting must be completed, if possible, before the east wind comes.

All of the men and boys, even some of the women, help with the planting. Shortly after sunrise they leave the village and scatter out to the many mesa-top fields. Food is brought to them by groups of young girls and the planting continues almost without interruption until sunset.

Planting methods are simple. A hole is dug, the seeds are dropped in, and the earth is pushed back into the hole. Light pressure with the foot compacts the moist soil about the seeds. Corn is planted almost a foot deep and a dozen or more kernels are placed in each hill. Beans and squash are given a shallower planting with fewer seeds in the hills. Sometimes the corn, beans and squash are planted in separate plots but often they are all planted together in the same field.

There are no rows, simply individual hills planted from five to eight feet apart with no effort toward orderliness. The only care exercised in the location of the hills is that they must not be in the same spot as those of last year. Enough stubs from the last year's crop have been left in place to indicate where not to plant. By changing the location of the hills each season and by wide planting the men save the soil, for it may be years before two hills are planted in the same spot.

The planting proceeds rapidly with the men digging the holes and the boys and girls dropping the seeds. Plot after plot is completed and the tension begins to lessen. In a few days every field is planted and the happy farmers sit back to wait for the rain. It is not long in coming. One evening the wind swings to the east and during the night the people are awakened by the pleasant sound of rain in the canyons. There are contented smiles on their faces as they are lulled back to sleep by the swishing waterfall that pours over the front of the cave.

The rain lasts for days. It is a soft, warm spring rain, a female rain. There is none of the bluster that will come with the male rains of late summer. Day and night it falls, and the earth, well-loosened by the winter frosts, drinks up the moisture.

There is happiness in Cliff Palace for an abundant harvest is now almost assured. The men gather in small groups along the front terraces, chatting gaily as they watch the rain. In their minds they see the grains of corn swell and burst, to send thin green shoots toward the light. In spite of the rain and mud some of them trot up to the mesa tops to look at the fields. They know exactly how the fields look but still they must see them. Nothing has happened. The earth is taking up the moisture, weeds are shooting out of the ground, but none of their plants have broken the surface. Drenched, they return to the cave to spread the word that all is well up on the mesa top.

The rainy days are days of rest for the men but they are days of strenuous activity for the women and girls. All of the great water jars must be filled and stored away. As soon as the spring rains are over the dry period will begin. It may be two months before there is another drop of rain so the storage of abundant supplies of water is of vital importance.

In the canyon below Cliff Palace is a series of dams. The first one is just below the trash pile at the front of the cave while the last one is far down the canyon. Several of the dams are quite large, five or six feet in height and over twenty feet in length. These dams are not like the farming terraces up on the mesas. They are for water storage, so they are kept cleaned out and are not allowed to silt up. Being made of large stones, chinked with smaller stones and adobe, they act as perfect barriers for the rain water that drains down the canyon. All of the dams have been cleaned out and repaired during the spring and the rain soon fills each one to overflowing. The great pools of water thus retained sometimes last the people of Cliff Palace until the summer rains come.

In addition to the storage pools the women also store great quantities of water in their jars. Hundreds of the large vessels have been made; each woman has several. As the rain sends streams of clear water cascading down the cliffs the women fill these jars and set them away in the cave, each one covered with a close-fitting stone lid. Scattered through the city are innumerable small rooms that are too small for living purposes. They are for the storage of corn and beans. Many of the rooms are still full of grain but some were emptied last winter and they now make a perfect place for storage of the precious jars of water. Long before the spring rains are over the jars are all filled and safely stored away.

As the rains begin to show signs of subsiding the men keep watchful eyes on the dams in the canyon. Some are built higher, others are strengthened so that when the rains cease and the dry weather begins they will be holding every possible drop of water. The great pools are shaded by cliffs and trees and they will keep the water cool and fresh far into the summer. With the water that is contained in the pools and the water jars, and the daily flow from nearby springs the people have little fear of water shortage.

After several days of almost continuous rain the skies clear and the sun beats down on a damp, green world. The warmth and moisture cause every growing thing to reach for the sky. Weeds spring up everywhere and after a few days the red soil of the fields is broken by the green shoots of sprouting plants. There is a splendid stand; the gods of fertility have heard the prayers of the people.

As spring slips into summer the people of Cliff Palace seem happy and contented. Everything indicates that a normal, prosperous year is in store for them and they should face it with light hearts. For the most part they do and during the spring there has been much gaiety and happiness in the town. But often the smiles are only on the surface – underneath is a deep, ever-present fear. Sometimes, when all goes well, this fear is almost forgotten. Then something happens and everyone is reminded of the evil beings who are always present – witches!

From earliest childhood each person has been taught to fear these creatures. Witches are evil human beings who have great supernatural power. They have only one desire – to harm and destroy people. Almost all diseases are caused by witches. They shoot objects into people whom they wish to harm; stones, rags, thorns, insects, bits of bone or even flesh from a corpse. Sometimes they even steal a person's heart. When a witch uses his power against anyone, death is the result unless a medicine man breaks the evil spell.

Witches may injure a person or they may work against the entire community. They bring on epidemics, they cause floods and high winds and they can even keep the rain from falling. A witch may not always be in human form; sometimes it takes the form of a dog, a coyote or an owl. But always it is a menace because of the desire to harm and destroy.

Only the medicine men can recognize witches and overpower them, for they have the same power as the witches. But the medicine men work for the people and there is a constant struggle between them and the evil beings. If a person is ill, the medicine man sucks out the object which a witch has shot into his body. If a witch steals someone's heart, the medicine man searches for it and restores it to the afflicted person.

Since the people of Cliff Palace know that witches are always present they try never to offend anyone. A next-door neighbor, even a member of one's own family, may be a witch and to offend him would be to invite disaster. Any person may be a witch so the people are suspicious of all unusual actions. If a man is jealous or constantly unhappy, if he roams about at night, or if he is seen lurking outside a house where someone is ill, he may find himself accused of witchcraft. For such a man life becomes a miserable affair. He is shunned by everyone and finally may be driven from the town. Or he may be punished severely and, if he persists in his evil ways, may be executed.

During the spring the witches have caused only a little trouble in the town. There has been some illness and a few people have died but it was nothing compared to what we shall see when winter comes. That is the time when the witches will be most active.

As spring ends the people are well satisfied with what they have accomplished for all the necessary work has been done. Houses have been repaired, new houses have been built and several young couples have married. Hunting has been good and the trading journeys, except for the loss of one party, were successful. Several new fields were cleared, much pottery was made and sufficient water is in storage. The fields have all been planted and, above all, the spring ceremonies have been performed.

The people of Cliff Palace are happy and contented as spring turns into summer.

5

SUMMER

Summer is an easy time for the people of Cliff Palace, a warm, lazy time. There are certain tasks to be performed but there is also much leisure time for sleeping in the shade, gossiping, gambling and trading. There is not the restless activity which was so evident during the spring. Life proceeds at a slow, easy pace.

The early summer is dry and warm. Little rain can be expected until in July; sometimes it does not come until August. The crops in the fields must live on the moisture stored in the earth and the people must live on the water they have stored in their pools and water jars, and the daily flow from the springs. Water is always the critical problem but this year conditions are very favorable.

June is often the hottest month of the summer. The sky is cloudless and the sun beats down day after day, drawing the moisture out of the earth. In the sun the temperature is high but the shade is cool and pleasant. The air is dry and a light breeze always blows across the mesa tops. The shade of even a small tree brings relief from the warmth of the sun.

Little clothing is worn. The women have small aprons of dangling yucca fiber strings while the men may wear loin-cloths of buckskin or cotton cloth. Children wear nothing at all. Yucca fiber sandals usually are worn by both men and women when they leave the cave but they are not essential about the city itself. The people of Cliff Palace are not clothes conscious and with their rich brown skins they need no protection from the sun. Even the men, who spend long hours in the sunny fields, need no covering.

The farmers are all smiles for their crops are growing prodigiously. Corn, beans and squash are growing well. Weeds are also prospering and the men pull them up or chop them out with their digging sticks. If the weeds are not destroyed, they take moisture that the crops need.

Every morning, not long after sunrise, the men trot up to the fields. For a few hours they work industriously, chopping weeds or loosening the soil around the plants. Earth is kept piled up around the stalks of corn. It was planted almost a foot deep and this heaping up of the earth around the hills puts the roots even farther underground. At that depth there is an abundance of moisture in the soil.

Along towards noon, when the sun is high over head and the heat becomes noticeable, the men end their labors. Some of them trot back down to the cave for a late breakfast. Others, whose fields are farther from the town, have brought their lunches and they spend the warm midday hours in the shade of the trees which border their fields.

These men have a deep, inborn love for farming. They are descended from a thousand years of successful farmers and a fanatical desire to make things grow is in their blood. They often go to the fields when there is nothing to be done. The weeds have been cut, the soil is well loosened, everything is just right. Still the men go to the fields to spend the hours among the growing things. Every hill of corn, every bean plant receives individual attention. Endlessly the men work about the fields, even though they only pick an occasional bug off the plants.

During the midday siesta the men often gather in little groups and while away the hours telling of crops of the past or dreaming of the harvest that is to come. Those hours are not always spent idly for there are many tasks the men can do as they sit in the shade. One man may chip arrowheads; another may whittle away on his new bow. Here a man is patching his sandals while his neighbor puts a new blade on his digging stick. Much can be accomplished during these hours when the sun is high and the shade is welcome.

The fields are never left without watchers. All day long someone is on guard and even during the night the young men and boys take turns watching the precious crops. Rabbits and squirrels eat the beans, and ravens and crows pull up the tender young corn plants. In a few hours a field can be ruined. Later on in the summer, crows, jays and ravens will tear at the ears of corn and eat great holes in the tender squashes. Even the coyotes like the squashes and as one of the animals trots through

Top. Modern Indian corn grown by ancient methods in the Mesa
     Verde experimental field
Bottom. Remains of terraces which provided garden plots for
     the early farmers

the field he may take great bites out of half a dozen. Faced with this danger, the farmers are forced to watch the fields day and night. The unmarried boys build brush shelters in the fields and spend much of the summer there, dreaming of the chubby little maidens for whom they will soon be farming.

The boys do not like to spend the night in the fields for witches are most active during the hours of darkness and it is a bad time to be away from the town. When a coyote howls or an owl hoots, they know it may be a witch so they throw more wood on their fires and smear ashes on their foreheads to keep the witches away.

As the dry weather of summer continues the people show much concern over the water supply. They know that if the late summer rains come normally, they will have more than enough. But if, as sometimes happens, the rains fail to come, they will be in serious trouble. They prepare for this possibility by carefully conserving the supplies. In order to save the water that is stored in the jars and in the pools below the cave the springs are utilized to the utmost. There are many of these springs along the canyon walls at the foot of the cliffs. One of the finest is across the canyon, under the great ceremonial building where the priests hold their most important ceremonies. It is almost half a mile by trail to the spring but it has a strong flow of water. In spite of the long, tiresome journey, the water must be saved. That is one of the tragedies in the lives of the men. They are forced to carry the water home from distant springs – on their wives' heads.

Each morning the women make the round of the springs to gather the water that has accumulated. At each place where there is a seepage they have made a basin of well-tamped blue shale. The water does not seep readily through this shale and a pool of clear water results. The best springs are visited several times a day so that the pools do not overflow. With their long-handled ladles the women dip the water into their jars, some of which hold as much as five gallons. The heavy jars are then borne home on their heads. Years of practice have given them strong necks, straight backs and a smooth, flowing stride. They chat happily as they trot home with their burdens: life is gay and easy with nothing to do but carry water up out of the canyon. By carrying the water jars on their heads the women have their hands free when they climb the rows of toe-holds that are cut into the more precipitous cliffs. Ladders that lead up over the terraced houses are simple: the water carriers trot up them without deigning to touch their hands to the poles.

Each woman has a small pad of yucca fibers, shaped like a large doughnut, which she places between her head and the water jar. This pad helps in balancing the burden and keeps her calloused head from cracking the precious jar.

Every effort is made to conserve the water supply, for as the warm weather continues the springs begin to dwindle and the pools shrink. There is no repairing and building of houses; water cannot be spared for the mortar. Pottery is seldom made at this time for that, too, requires water. By using it only for human needs the supply can be drawn out for months if necessary.

In addition to their water carrying activities the women are also busy gathering the edible plants that are so common during the summer. These plants add variety to the diet and help to conserve the stores of grain. In June the mesa tops are covered with flowers of all kinds and the women admire them and call them by name as they search for the plants that have value as food or medicine. The leaves and fruit of the prickly pear are eaten; also the beautiful waxy flowers and the tender flower stem of the yucca. Lily bulbs, wild onions, beeweed, sumac berries and Mormon tea are only a few of the natural products which the women gather. They know every seed, root, bulb, berry and plant that has value and they search the mesas and canyons in order to obtain these additional foods and flavors.

Occasionally the women interrupt the usual routine of their daily tasks in order to give birth to babies. It is a pleasant diversion for children are highly prized in this society. A woman continues her regular work almost until time for the happy event. Being strong and active she ordinarily goes through it without great difficulty. Her mother is in charge of the affair but if all does not go well, a medicine man is called in to chant her through her troubles.

Shortly after birth the baby is bathed and is rubbed with juniper ashes to protect it from witches and other evil influences. It is then placed on a bed of hot sand and a perfect ear of corn is kept always beside it. For twenty days the mother and child are kept in the house away from strong light and every fifth day the mother's hair is washed with yucca suds and she is bathed with water in which juniper twigs have been boiled.

At sunrise on the twentieth day the child's head is washed. Then its grandmother on its father's side takes it to the top of the cliff and with a little ceremony of prayer, dedicates it to the Sun Father. On this day it is named and since all of its aunts and both grandmothers have the privilege of giving it a name, the baby may receive a dozen. One name finally wins out and the others are forgotten.

For several months the child is kept on a cradle board most of the time. This is merely a thin, smooth board to which the child is bound with soft folds of cotton cloth or buckskin and a lacing of strings. No pillow is provided and the soft, pliable head rests on the hard board month after month. The result is obvious. Gradually the back of the head flattens until it fits the board.

This change of head shape has no effect on the child except in the matter of appearance. As the skull presses in at the back it bulges out over the ears. The brain adjusts itself to the changing shape of its container and suffers no ill effects. As a result of the use of this hard cradle board, all of the people have the deformity on the back of the head. Sometimes it is terrific and the head is as wide as it is long.

The cradle board makes the care of the child very simple. The mother may carry it on her back as she goes about her work. She may hang it on a tree or on a roof pole or lean it up against the house. When the child is on its cradle board it is in no danger of rolling off the roof or over a cliff. Occasionally it is taken off the cradle and the juniper bark pad that serves as a diaper is changed. When the child reaches the age where it must learn to walk, it will be released from the cradle and will be placed in the constant care of an older sister or some other little girl of its clan.

For the first six or seven years, children lead carefree lives. They have no responsibilities and nothing is expected of them except that they survive and be happy. If they do wrong they are seldom punished physically but are talked to at great length. And quite often they are frightened into good behavior by tales of witches and what they do to bad children.

All of the children are up at dawn and the day's play begins. The very young ones must stay within the cave where they climb over the houses and play on the roofs and in the courts. After they are a little older they play on the canyon slope below the cave and finally they are big enough to play along the cliffs beside the town. All through the day the echoes of their voices and laughter fill the canyon.

At the age of six or seven, this life of constant play ends and they begin to learn, by imitating their parents, all they must know to fit into the life of the community. A little girl follows her mother wherever she goes and imitates her in every activity. When the mother makes pottery her small daughter makes crude, miniature pieces: when the mother bakes corn cakes her little shadow bakes tiny cakes of mud and, after a time, is allowed to use the precious corn meal itself. When the mother goes to the spring the little girl trots at her heels and soon she is carrying small jars of water on her head. She spends long hours at the grinding bin and equally long hours caring for younger brothers and sisters. As she grows older, she accepts more and more responsibility and finally, when marriage comes, she is an accomplished housewife.

In the same manner the small boy goes through a long period of training. At sunrise he tumbles out of his blankets to listen and watch attentively as his father says his morning prayer and tosses an offering of corn meal or corn pollen to the gods of dawn. He follows his father to the fields and as soon as he is old enough, accompanies him on hunting trips. When his father makes bows, arrows, flint knives, bone awls and the many other tools, the boy imitates him, in miniature, and gradually learns all the necessary crafts.

Most important of all to the youth is his religious education and this is in the hands of his "ceremonial father." When the boy was born one of his mother's brothers was selected for this task and he is responsible for the religious training of his young nephew. The two spend long hours together as the uncle tells the legends and beliefs of the tribe. Since there is no written language, these can be learned only through hearing them repeated over and over. During the first years of training the boy learns only the general things which all the people may know but when he is twelve or fourteen he is ready for the secret part of his religious training. Under the sponsorship of his "ceremonial father" he is taken into one of the kivas and initiated into the secret society to which his "ceremonial father" belongs. Now he is taught the secrets of the society and its ceremonies and soon he begins to take part in the ceremonial work. From this time on the kiva plays an important part in the young man's life. He goes there not only for ceremonial purposes but to work, loaf, gamble or even to sleep. If his mother's house is crowded with younger children, he may sleep in his kiva most of the time until he marries. And even after marriage he may sleep within the safe confines of the kiva during occasional periods of strife in his home.

As the dry weather continues the men keep an anxious eye on the sky. Certain conditions must develop before the rains can come. In June there is a sigh of relief from the farmers. The sky is no longer a solid canopy of blue. Along the northeastern horizon great white clouds begin to appear. At first they are small but each day they grow larger. Soon they are tremendous, billowy, white thunderheads that boil up until they cover half the sky. Soon they will break and the worries of the farmers will be over.

The crops are growing well. By the end of June the corn is almost knee high and the men thin it out. The weak stalks are pulled out of each hill leaving the five or six strongest ones. The fight against weeds is continued but during most of the summer the men have a great deal of time for other activities.

During the times when they are not completely occupied with their farms they work at their various crafts and as a result there is much trading. Each man needs certain things such as turkey feather blankets, cotton blankets, jewelry, tanned buckskin, sandals, leggings, bows, arrows, planting sticks, stone knives and scrapers, yucca fiber cords and ropes, axes, hammers, and countless other things. Some of the men can and do make any or all of these things. Most of the men, however, specialize on the things they can do best and trade for their other necessities.

In one house lives a man who makes splendid arrowheads. Next door is an old fellow who is famous for his cotton blankets. Upstairs is an axe maker and still higher, in the third story house, is a man who specializes in tanning buckskin. Across the court is a young fellow who is especially adept at twisting yucca fibers into cords and ropes. In another part of the city is one who makes feather blankets; somewhere else is a jeweler. Some of the men make a number of different things but few of them make all of the items they need.

The result of this semi-specialization is that there is much trading. This is true not only within Cliff Palace but also between the various villages. Within a mile of the large city are more than thirty cliff dwellings. Up the canyon to the north are ten and directly across the canyon, within easy calling distance, are two very small ones. Around the point behind the great, mesa-top, ceremonial building are five, down the canyon are eleven and in the next canyon to the east are several more. In more distant canyons are hundreds of other villages, large and small.

Trails lead from one to the next and when a man needs something he trots off to the place where he knows he can find it. He spends the day at his trading even though he needs only a single stone knife. He may visit two or three men who make knives, haggling with each. In between times he gossips with friends. When meal time comes he pulls up beside any convenient food bowl and is a welcome though uninvited guest. After overeating he takes a nap, then returns to his trading. Toward the end of the day he makes a deal and sets out for home. The same bargain could have been made early in the morning but that would have robbed him of all the day's pleasure.

Since Cliff Palace is so large it is the scene of much trading, for men from the smaller villages can find anything they want somewhere in the city. Early in the morning they come trotting up the trail to spend the day in the cool shadowy cave trading for what they need. When the heat of the day is over they set out for home with their new possessions.

Sometimes men of other tribes come to trade and there is great excitement in the city. The strangers not only bring beautiful jewelry and much-needed cotton and salt but they bring news from the outside world. This is almost as important as

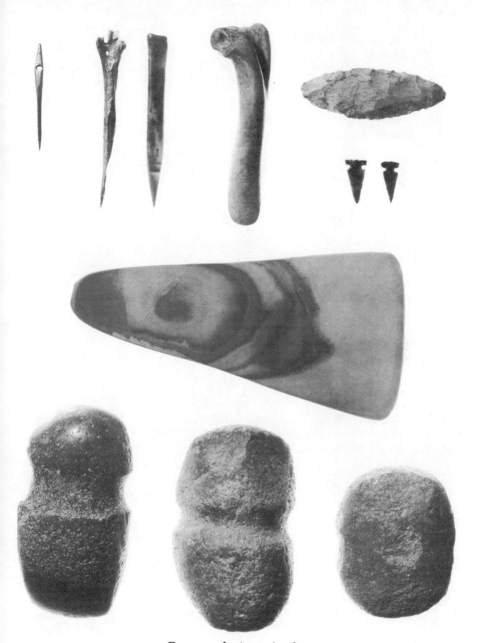

Bone and stone tools

Top. Bone needle, bone awls, bone scraper, stone knife and
      arrowheads
Middle. Highly polished stone blade
Bottom. Stone axe, hammer and hammerstone

the actual objects of trade and before the trading can begin, the people must hear what is going on outside their own little world.

The news that the welcome traders bring is of an infinite variety. It may concern the weather, the crops, the hunting conditions, or the private affairs of the people. The news may be bad: somewhere a village has been visited by a scourge of dysentery and half of the children are dead; in one region a plague of grasshoppers has destroyed the crops; somewhere else a forest fire has wiped out the entire population; in another place the enemy tribes are becoming stronger and village after village is being wiped out. There is no joy when these things are told. But more often the news is good: there is a fine crop of pinon nuts on a distant mountain; in a certain region the deer are as thick as lice on an old man's head; a new vein of turquoise has been discovered that yields hard, blue stones. Much of the news is of a personal nature: there has been a murder; in a certain village a woman has had triplets; a man has been thrown out by his mother-in-law because he snored too loudly; a certain priest is having miraculous luck with his healing ceremonies; a deformed child has been born; a well-known chief has gone blind.

Much of the news is pure gossip and it is repeated time after time, gaining spice and details with each telling. There is no restraint in discussions concerning intimate personal affairs and every new bit of scandal is relished by the fireside listeners. The travelers who bring news from distant regions expect an even trade for they must return home with a full stock of news for their own people.

The news which has the greatest effect upon the listeners is that concerning the enemy raiders. For generations the threat has been increasing. So far the Mesa Verde has not suffered but the people know the danger is coming closer each year. There are so many villages on the great, protective mesa that they have always felt safe. In the caves are hundreds of cliff dwellings, all easily defended, and since each village is within shouting distance of the next, help could quickly be summoned. But the savage raiders grow bolder and stronger. Sooner or later they will come climbing up to the top of the Mesa Verde to steal women and corn, even though it is a long way to go for corn.

Except for these alarming bits of news, the visits of the traders are festive occasions. Everyone marvels at the things they bring. The men bargain endlessly and the exchange of news continues day after day. The women cook their finest dishes and the dusty travelers are honored guests. After days of friendly visiting and trading, they start back down the trail bearing the good wishes of the people of Cliff Palace.

Gambling is also a common indulgence among the men and much of the exchange of goods is through gambling rather than trading. At any time of the day a knot of interested onlookers can be seen somewhere in the city, silently watching some game of change. Anything that has the slightest value can be gambled. The stakes may be only insignificant objects, or a man may stake everything he possesses against a single fine piece of jewelry. It may be a guessing contest, a game of skill, or a pure game of chance in which small carved bones are thrown on the floor and the winner is determined by the manner in which the bones turn up. Someone wins, someone loses, and no one is hurt. By a few days of diligent labor a man can replace any of the things lost, except jewelry, which has the greatest value of any of his possessions. Necklaces, pendants, and earrings are made of turquoise, colored stones and sea shells. Some of them are exquisite: the beads of turquoise or stone are sometimes so fine that there are thousands of them on a single necklace. Such a necklace requires weeks of painstaking labor.

Toward the middle of July there is an ominous threat in the air each afternoon. Billowing thunderheads fill the sky and turn to a dark angry shade. Sudden gusts of wind rip across the mesa tops threatening to uproot the corn and there is a distant roll of thunder. The air is heavy and depressing. Each day the skies become darker. Except for the men who are watching fields, the people stay close to the cave. No one wants to be far from shelter when the storm breaks.

At last the day comes. By noon the sky is filled with heavy clouds. Shortly afternoon there is a sudden roar of wind. Cannonading crashes of thunder echo constantly through the canyons and searing tongues of lightning flick the treetops. Suddenly, all is still. Not a leaf stirs; the world is breathless. The storm draws back its arm for one quiet moment, then mercilessly lashes the earth with floods of rain. Wind, thunder and lightning resume and for a noisy hour the mesas bow their heads under the wrath of the elements.

A roaring waterfall shoots out over the front of Cliff Palace cave and from the bottom of the canyon comes the roar of a rushing stream. The people are silent as they watch the storm from their sheltered housetops. There is joy in their hearts, for the rain ends all worries, but there is an ominous note in the terrible fury of the storm. The male rains of summer are often like this. They make a great show of noise and power, far different from the gentle female rains of spring.

In an hour the storm ends as suddenly as it began. The rain stops, the clouds break up and the sun beams down on a dripping world.

Immediately the men are off to the fields to see if the crops have suffered. The drenched watchers, whose brush shelters were poor protection against the storm, assure them that little damage has been done. Some of the corn is down but it will straighten up. The only real loss is that a few terraces have washed out but that is not serious for the terrace crops are important only in dry years when the mesa-top fields fail.

There is great rejoicing in Cliff Palace. The harvests are assured for now that the rains have started they will continue. Every few days for the rest of the summer there will be a rain, sometimes heavy, sometimes light. The danger of water shortage is definitely ended. All of the pools are full of fresh water and the springs will soon flow with renewed vigor as the rain water reaches them. There is water in abundance and the people no longer need to use it so sparingly.

With the arrival of the rains the heat is broken. The days are cooler now and large, fluffy clouds float about the sky, sending their cool shadows racing across the earth. The nights are sometimes so cool that a feather blanket is necessary for comfort.

As July turns into August the people are happy and contented. All goes well; there are no threats to their security. The fields are bursting with growth and the springs are flowing freely. Those are the two important things in their lives. There is no press of work at this time of the year and life is easy. The men watch the fields and work leisurely at their various crafts. The women still gather plants for food and now that there is an abundance of water they make a little pottery and repair their houses.

As always, the children are restless and active. They imitate their elders, doing everything in miniature; miniature farms, miniature bows and arrows, miniature houses and miniature pottery. Sometimes they capture young animals; birds, chipmunks, squirrels or rabbits and while away the hours in more or less unsuccessful efforts to tame them. They are never without their dogs and as they play about the canyons they keep watchful eyes on their flocks of turkeys lest they stray too far and fall prey to coyotes and foxes.

Life is full of joy for these children. Day after day they do nothing but play Indian!

During the summer there is only one threat to the happiness and security of the people. Only by terrific effort are the medicine men able to avert a calamity that would wipe out the entire population. One afternoon a terrified scream comes from the small cliff dwelling across the canyon and a man is seen dancing about on the cliff, waving his arms and pointing frantically toward the sun.

Alarmed, the men shade their eyes and look at the sun as best they can. Immediately they realize the awful calamity that threatens them. Half of the sun has turned black; some frightful monster is swallowing the Sun God. If it succeeds the world will become dark and cold. Life will end.

Instantly the priests go into action and from the kivas come the sounds of their frenzied chanting. Offerings are made, prayers are sung: they perform every magic trick they know that might force the monster to spit out the sun. Everyone in the village joins in and the men come running from the fields. Only a disaster like this could force them to leave the precious crops. For a frenzied hour the hysterical people call upon their gods to drive away the monster that threatens their Sun God.

For a time the blot on the sun grows larger, then, as the priests redouble their efforts, it begins to diminish. At last it is gone and the exhausted people give thanks to their gods. Once again the power of the priests has saved them.

This thing has happened often, sometimes to the sun, sometimes to the moon. Only a few years ago the monster swallowed the moon completely. The oldest men can remember a time when the sun was swallowed completely and the earth grew dark. But in each case the power of the medicine men prevailed and the moon and sun returned undiminished.

Emergencies of this kind give the people renewed faith in their priests. Sometimes they fail to produce rain or cure the sick but such failures can be overlooked when they are able to overpower a demon which threatens the very existence of the people. Never yet have they lost the battle against this demon which threatens to swallow the moon or the sun. Surely their power is supreme.

Throughout the year the priests have a regular round of ceremonies. Fall and early winter is the great ceremonial season but there are certain ceremonies that must be performed at other times. Healing ceremonies are performed whenever there is need. In the spring the fertility rites must be conducted and during the summer certain ceremonies must be performed which will cause the gods to send rain. In a dry year these rain ceremonies are of utmost importance but in years like this one, when the rains have already come, the ceremonies are more in the nature of thanksgiving. Even though the gods have sent the rain the ceremonies are performed. If they were neglected the gods would be offended.

When the prescribed date arrives the elaborate ceremonies begin. For days there are secret ceremonies in the kiva of the religious society that conducts this particular rite. As a climax the tired priests come out of the secret chamber and perform the public part of the ceremony. Housetops are crowded as the people gather to watch the costumed priests go through the ritual that has been handed down through countless generations of priests. Year after year it is the same but the people never tire of it. Every chant, every offering, every bit of action has a meaning. It is all a part of the yearly cycle of ceremonies that brings happiness and prosperity to the people. This ceremonial cycle is the responsibility of the priests and the people have profound confidence in their abilities.

The people also have great confidence in their chiefs and in the members of the council for these men govern the town. The most important official is the Town Chief, an elderly man who is noted for his wisdom, patience and understanding. He knows many chants and ceremonies which help his people. Next in importance is the War Chief, who guards against enemies, witches and quarrels within the town. The Sun Chief or Sun Watcher follows the movements of the sun and keeps the yearly calendar, and his observations determine the dates for many of the ceremonies. The Hunt Chief is in charge of the hunting activities of the town as well as important healing and hunting ceremonies. Another official who is prominent throughout the year is the Crier Chief. He is the town crier and from his roof he announces important news events and the dates of ceremonies, village hunts and other important affairs.

In addition to these chiefs, there is a council composed of the head men, or chiefs, of all the secret societies. When there are problems to be settled, the council meets: perhaps someone is accused of witchcraft, perhaps two clans are quarreling over farm lands, or it may be merely a personal quarrel between two men. A council meeting is called and the town chiefs and the members of the council meet in a kiva with all the interested parties. A council meeting may last for hours and there is much shouting and quarreling as the evidence is presented. After each person has had an opportunity to give his evidence and opinions the Town Chief makes his decision and the trouble is over. The Town Chief is considered to be wise and just and his judgments are never questioned.

As the end of summer draws near there is new excitement around the cooking fires and in the fields. It is green corn time and the tender ears of corn are at last ready for use. The corn plants are now as high as a man's head and although the ears are fully formed, the kernels are tender and milky. They are still white: the brilliant colors will not appear until they begin to harden later on. Each day as the men come home from the fields they bring baskets of corn to their wives. The fresh corn is roasted, baked, boiled or stewed and great quantities are eaten when the families gather around their food bowls for the evening meal. Much of this green corn is also prepared for winter use. It is roasted, ground into fine meal and carefully stored away. When winter comes it will be made into delicious mush and a thin gruel which will serve as a hot drink.

Just as summer slips into autumn the corn fields are the scene of a gay festival. Each day the men have examined the ears and now that they are just right, the date is set. The Crier Chief steps out on his roof, which overlooks the entire town, and gaining the attention of the people, announces that the green corn festival will be held in two days. His announcement brings a great flurry of excitement and the women begin to prepare for the feasting which will take place.

On the appointed day all who are able to climb the steep trails hurry to the fields. Yesterday the men dug deep pits in the fields and gathered great quantities of firewood. Hundreds of ears of corn were picked and placed near the pits. Last night fires were started in the pits and all through the night fuel was thrown in to keep the fires roaring.

As the people arrive from the village the fires are allowed to die out and the ashes are scraped out of the superheated pits. Green corn stalks and leaves are used to line each pit and everyone gathers around to toss in the hundreds of ears of un-shucked, green corn. When a pit is almost full, more corn stalks are tossed in and the pit is sealed with earth. All through the day the corn steams in the huge ovens.

Small fires are built around the edges of the fields and the women and girls spend the day preparing great quantities of food. The children romp about the fields while wrestling contests, races and games of skill occupy the boys and young men. The older men loaf and talk and, of course, gamble a little. As the day passes the excitement mounts and at last, as the cool evening breeze begins to rustle the corn leaves, the feasting begins.

The pits are opened and the steaming, tender ears are passed out to the famished crowd. It is a joyous feast for green corn is a favorite delicacy. Great quantities of food are consumed and a contented silence settles over the gorged, happy people.

Just as a monstrous full moon rises out of the eastern mesa they return to their homes. They thrill at the sight for it is something many of them seldom see. Cliff Palace cave faces west and they can see the full moon only by climbing to the mesa top.

With the green corn festival over, summer slips quickly into autumn. The slow, easy days of the growing season are over. The strenuous activity of the harvest season faces the people of Cliff Palace.

6

AUTUMN

With the arrival of autumn the finest weather of the year begins. For almost three months it will continue, until winter sweeps down out of the north. In early September the days are still warm but the nights have a pleasant coolness. As the season progresses the daytime warmth continues but the nights become cooler and cooler. By October they are crisp and finally there is frost. The mesas flame with the colors of autumn, the distant mountains are cloaked with a bluegray haze and for weeks the people enjoy the brisk invigorating weather of Indian Summer. Late in October, or in November, there may be a quick flurry of snow, a warning of what is to come, but it disappears as quickly as it came. Far into the autumn the warm days last: sometimes the winter storms do not begin until after the sun has started to return from the south.

Autumn is the happiest season of the year for the people of the Mesa Verde. It is a season of tremendous activity for now they must reap the rewards for the prayers of springtime and the labors of summer. During the spring they were gay and happy but it was not the full unrestrained happiness of autumn. As the farmers planted their crops last spring they felt a certain helplessness. With each tiny seed they planted a prayer: that was the only aid they could give it. Then they were forced to stand by while the forces of nature; the sun, the rain and the earth, did as they pleased with the precious seeds.

Autumn has brought the rewards for their prayers and labors. There is no uncertainty about it. Nature has smiled, the fields have prospered and nothing can rob them of a bountiful harvest. The cooling weather is turning the fields yellow and a period of strenuous activity will soon begin. Every grain of corn, every bean, every squash must be carried down to the cave and stored safely away.

The fields are never left unattended. Ravens, crows and jays try to get at the corn in the daytime and deer get into the fields at night unless they are guarded. All through the night

97

bright fires burn in the fields as the men and boys take turns protecting the crops. As they walk about the fields they gloat over the success of their farming efforts. The corn is higher than their heads and heavy ears bend toward the ground. The bean vines are full of fat pods and the fields are dotted with great yellowing squashes. It will be a wonderful harvest; the fields are full of song and laughter as the proud farmers rejoice over their success.

Even before the main harvest starts, the products begin to trickle down to the cave. There is an abundance of help for even the children and women join in. Each plant is given individual attention and when an ear of corn, a bean pod or a squash ripens too soon, it is picked and carried home.

As the first light frosts of October begin to bring color to the mesas the harvest is on. Everyone helps and from dawn until dusk the trails are full of happy carriers as the fields pour their products into Cliff Palace. Many of the fields are far off across the mesa tops and in a day's time each person can make only a few trips.

A single, fat slippery squash is all that can be carried at one time and it takes only a few large ears of corn to fill a basket. Dozens of trips are required in harvesting even a small field. Early in the morning the carriers trot down the trails but as the day wears on the pace becomes slower.

Some of the corn is husked in the fields and only the ears are carried home but much of it is snapped off the stalks and taken home to be husked later. Sometimes the stalks are cut and the entire plant is carried down to the cave for the stalks, leaves, tassels and shucks are used in many ways. Beans usually are threshed in the fields. The dry pods are piled on a plot of hard, smooth ground and the women beat them with long sticks until the beans are freed. Then the whole mass of beaten pods is poured from baskets held high above their heads and the breeze blows the chaff away, leaving only the clean beans. Sometimes the beans are picked and carried down to the cave for threshing but that is more difficult for in the cave there is no breeze to blow away the chaff.

As the harvest progresses, Cliff Palace becomes a parade of color. Everything must be spread out on the roofs and in the courts to dry and soon the people can scarcely move about. The corn is brilliantly tinted; red, black, blue, yellow, white and speckled, and the city becomes a flaming riot of colors. Corn is everywhere. It is piled high on the roof tops, it is spread out in every court and long strings of brilliant ears hang from the ends of roof poles. Piles of rich brown beans and waxy yellow and green squashes add to the color and the confusion. The terraced houses of Cliff Palace are now solid banks of color and still the harvest continues.

Like busy brown ants the women and girls move about the throbbing city. From morning until night they are busy shucking corn, threshing beans, braiding strings of corn, turning the corn and beans each day so they dry properly, and finally storing them away in the bins. The storage of supplies is always a responsibility of the women. While the things were growing in the fields they belonged to the men but now that they have been harvested and brought down to the city, they have become the women's property. The women of each household, which is a group of families, store their foodstuffs in common and apportion them out to the various families as they are needed.

Some of the corn is shelled and stored in baskets but most of it is stored on the cob. The different colors are sorted out and the bright ears are stacked like cordwood. The beans must be stored in baskets and jars but the squashes can be piled anywhere. Many of the squashes are peeled and cut into long strips. After the strips have dried they are rolled up in bundles and stored away. In the winter, soaking will restore the flavor of the fresh squash.

High up in the back of the cave is a long, narrow crevice containing a dozen large storage rooms and throughout the town there are many more. They have been chinked carefully against rats and mice and each one is lined with dry corn leaves and tassels to protect the grain from dampness. One after another these rooms are filled and the doors are sealed.

When the harvest finally ends there are enough beans and corn in storage to last not only until the next harvest, but on through two or three years if coming harvests should fail. By carefully conserving the supplies the people could survive two or three seasons of drouth. That is the possibility for which they must always be prepared, for normal harvests do not come every year.

All through the harvest the workers have watched for perfect ears of corn and when found they were put aside. These will be saved for seed and they are stored separately in the safest, driest places. Even though planting time is months away small ceremonies are performed over these precious ears.

Although the agricultural products are of first importance to the people of Cliff Palace, there are in addition countless wild products that they must gather and store away. Throughout the autumn, when they are not busy with their harvest, they search the mesas and canyons for these natural foodstuffs. Corn, beans, and squash would be a tiresome diet so meat, nuts, roots, fruit, seeds and berries are needed.

This year there is a splendid crop of pinon nuts and the women and children are busy gathering them. The early frosts have opened the cones and the ground under each pinon tree is covered with brown nuts that are scarcely larger than beans. Squirrels, chipmunks and Indians engage in a lively contest for them but there are more than enough for all. They are stored away in baskets to be eaten later in the winter. Usually they are cracked one at a time with the teeth and eaten raw but sometimes they are ground, shell and all, into an oily butter and eaten with corn bread. Pinon nuts are highly prized but they cannot be depended upon regularly. Sometimes several years elapse between crops.

In addition to pinon nuts many other plant products are gathered, dried and stored for the winter. Yucca pods, cactus fruits, berries, roots and seeds all have their uses. Medicinal herbs are also gathered as well as plants that will be needed for dying cotton cloth and buckskin. Bundles of drying plants hang on the walls of every house.

During the summer there was little hunting, for the deer and mountain sheep drifted north into the higher country. Now they are returning and as soon as the harvest is over, the men begin to lay in the winter's supply of meat. Hunting parties vary in size from one man to all of the men in the town and there are always important ceremonial preparations. Prayer

Top. Corn is husked and spread on the roofs to dry
Bottom. The man who cut the log too short

sticks are made, prayers are said and each man carries a tiny stone image of some animal, such as the mountain lion, which is a good hunter. When the organized town hunts are planned, the hunt society holds ceremonies in its kiva the night before the hunt begins. Unless these ceremonial preparations are made, a hunt cannot be successful. If a man were to neglect the ceremonies it would be worse than if he were to forget to take his weapons.

If one man or a small party of men goes out after deer or mountain sheep, they usually stalk the animals and shoot them with their bows and arrows. The men know the game trails and waterholes and by careful, patient stalking, they are able to get within shooting distance. If deer skins are needed for ceremonial purposes, the men run the animals down and choke them to death for ceremonial skins must not be pierced by arrows. When a deer finds that it is being pursued, it becomes too nervous to eat or drink. As the man follows it hour after hour he imitates the cries of coyotes or wolves and after a time the animal is frightened to the point of exhaustion and the man is able to catch it, throw it down and choke it to death.

Dates for the organized hunts, in which all of the men of the town take part, are set by the Hunt Chief and announced by the Crier Chief. When the large groups of men go hunting they either drive the game out on a high point between two canyons or form a large circle and drive the game to the center. The mesa south of Cliff Palace is an excellent place for a game drive for it is narrow and the cliffs are very high. When the Hunt Chief learns that deer or mountain sheep are on this mesa, a hunt is announced and early the next morning the men leave the town. Forming a long line across the mesa they drive the game toward the point. The cliffs are so high the animals cannot leave the mesa top and soon they are cornered on the point of the mesa with a solid line of men blocking their escape. The animals are killed with arrows and clubs and any that dash over the cliff are picked up below.

When a surround hunt has been announced the men go north on the mesa to areas where game is especially plentiful. The easiest way is for them to split into two parties and move up two canyons which are parallel. When a signal is given the men swarm up out of the canyons and form a circle which at first may be a mile in diameter. With much shouting they move toward the center and soon all the deer, mountain sheep, foxes, coyotes, and rabbits which were in the area are surrounded by a tight circle of men. As the frightened animals try to dash out of the circle they are killed with arrows and clubs.

When hunting parties return the game is turned over to the women and girls. The animals are skinned and the meat is cut into long strips. Strings are tied to pegs in the house walls and to the ends of roof beams and soon the houses are festooned with drying meat. Almost every part of an animal is used. The meat and most of the internal organs are eaten, the hide is tanned for clothing, sinews are used for bow strings and for sewing and the bones are made into tools. All through the late fall, hunting continues and for weeks the cave reeks with the strong odor of drying meat.

Throughout the fall the harvesting and hunting activities occupy the people of Cliff Palace. When evening comes they are tired from their labors but they are happy as they sit around the fires which have been lighted to drive off the chill. They face the winter with light hearts for the walls are bulging with the supplies of food that have been stored away.

It is the same all over the Mesa Verde. In every cliff dwelling there is contentment. This has been a good year for the entire tribe and the people are enjoying the reward that has come from their labors.

Even though the strenuous harvest days are over the people are still busy. A cold winter is coming and preparations must be made for it. When December and January come there will be snow and ice. Bitter winds will sweep across the mesa and the shadowy depths of the cave will be cold. An abundance of warm clothing will be required if the people are to enjoy any comfort during the winter.

The most important articles of clothing are the feather blankets. Weaving them is a slow, tedious task but they are splendid protection against the cold. In making a feather blanket only two things are used; small, fluffy turkey feathers and heavy, yucca cord. The feathers are split down the middle and wrapped in a very tight spiral around the cord. A soft, fluffy feather rope results; hundreds of feet are needed for a single blanket. When enough of the feather rope has been made, it is woven into a blanket that is as soft and warm as a fur robe. The men who make these blankets are busy making new ones and repairing old ones. Each person will need one when cold weather comes.

Other men weave new cotton blankets and some of the boys are sent off to the south for more cotton. Cotton robes are not as warm as those made of feathers but they give added warmth when they are worn next to the skin under the feather blankets. When a feather blanket is old and worn some of the feather ends loosen and a cotton under-blanket is needed to prevent scratching.

Deer and mountain sheep skins are tanned into soft white leather. By using bone awls and needles the women sew the skins together with yucca fiber or cotton string and make large robes. A few sleeveless slip-over buckskin jackets are made but most of the people prefer the loose robes. Yucca fiber sandals are worn throughout the year but in the winter grass and juniper bark are sometimes bound to the foot by the sandal lacings and extra warmth is provided. Short leggings, made from buckskin or woven of human hair, are often worn by the men when they leave the cave.

As winter draws near and the threat of cold weather comes close the people check their clothing needs carefully. Each man, woman and child will need certain things so the weaving and sewing continue until everyone is well supplied. With the bountiful supplies of food, an abundance of fuel, and a good stock of clothing the people are able to face the dreary months of winter with less dread. They hate to see winter come for there will be suffering and sadness. But only winter can lead to spring so they must accept it.

In the late fall, when the rush of harvest is over and the preparations for winter are well under way, the men begin to think of ceremonies. This is the season for the greatest ceremonial activity and the men are often busy carrying out the rituals that are prescribed by their elaborate ceremonial calendar.

At almost any time of the year a ceremony of some kind is going on in Cliff Palace. It may be only a simple bit of ritual occupying a single medicine man or it may be an elaborate ceremony that occupies an entire religious society for many days. The priests of each society have a ceremonial calendar and as the seasons roll around they perform their ancient rituals. When, why and how those ceremonies originated they do not know. They learned them from their elders and they will pass them on to the younger men who will succeed them.

Throughout the year many ceremonies are held but the important ceremonial season comes in the late fall and winter. The work of spring, summer and fall is over and the men now have ample time for the involved rituals that keep them in tune with the powers that control the universe. These powers, or gods, are many and varied and strangely, they are both good and bad. The effort of the priests, then, is to call upon the good gods to help the people and to influence the bad gods to leave them alone.

Most important of all the powers is the Sun, who is the Father, and closely allied is the Earth Mother. In addition there are gods who control rain, growth of plants, fertility, the flow of springs and countless other things. Added to these are innumerable lesser supernatural beings who can help or harm the people. All nature is full of powers and it is the business of the medicine men to keep the whole complicated system in tune. It is not so much a worship of the forces of nature as a recognition of these forces. If they work smoothly together, life flows evenly and properly. If there is discord among the natural forces the people suffer. To them it means that some god is not pleased. The result is drouth, pestilence, famine, or any of the other curses that occasionally fall upon them.

In order to explain all of the acts of nature which influence the people, there is a tremendous mass of legends and myths. The origin of the universe and the origin of all life, including the people themselves, is contained in these myths. For every condition or act of nature there is an involved mythological explanation. The medicine men must keep this legendary background in order and they must faithfully carry out the yearly program of ceremonies. One of their most important duties is the training of the younger men. Just as they themselves received the myths and rituals from their elders so must they in turn pass them on to the men who will follow them.

In each generation a certain number of the men are concerned almost entirely with religious matters. They are the
medicine men, or priests, to whom is entrusted the responsibility of the delicate adjustments between man and the forces
of nature. Each religious society has one or more full-fledged
medicine men and a number of younger men who are learning
the profession. In addition, all of the other men of the society
know a great deal about the mythological background and the
ceremonies. Consequently, the men spend a great deal of
time in religious work.

Cliff Palace has twenty-three kivas and a large number of
secret religious societies. All of the societies have the same
general beliefs and background but each society splits off from
the main mythological stem and has certain phases of the religious work to carry out. The function of the various societies
is to control the weather, bring rain, promote fertility and
crops, assure successful hunts, control the sun and the seasons,
cure sickness, combat witches and promote the general welfare
of the people.

When a boy is twelve or fourteen years of age, he is initiated
into one of the societies, usually into the one to which his
"ceremonial father" belongs. This "ceremonial father" is the
uncle who was chosen to be the boy's adviser and sponsor and
it is natural for the boy to follow him. The uncles on the
mother's side are in many ways closer to a boy than is his own
father. The father belongs to a different clan and while he lives
with his family, in his wife's house, he spends a great deal of
time with his own clan group where he may be the "ceremonial
father" of one of his small nephews. Since marriage cannot
take place between two members of the same clan the father
is, to a certain extent, an outsider who has little to do with the
religious training of his sons. Maternal uncles take the father's
place in this matter.

During the fall, the initiation ceremonies take place and the
training of the boys begins. They must learn the legends, the
rituals and the endless chants so they can bear their share of
the ceremonial work. The few boys who are selected to be
medicine men will do little else but sit at the feet of the older
medicine men for a score of years. When their teachers die,
they will be able to step into their places.

The initiation and the training take place in the kivas. Night after night, through the fall and winter, the great cave resounds with the chants of the priests as they perform the ceremonies or teach them to the newly initiated members. Much of the legendary material is in the form of endless songs and the men never tire of them. Hour after hour they sit around the kiva fires, eyes closed, chanting softly the musical prayers and legends. Often the chanting continues through the night: now that the season's strenuous work is over the men are able to spend the nights with their ceremonies and rest in the daytime.

Most of the activities of a society take place in its kiva, which is a ceremonial room, work shop, club room and often, a sleeping chamber. During most of the year it serves as a club room for the men. When the time for a ceremony arrives it becomes a sacred, religious chamber. After the conclusion of the ceremony it is again a loafing place and work room. Women usually enter the kivas only on occasions when they take part in the ceremonies, or are invited in to witness them.

An unmarried boy, after being initiated, often sleeps in the kiva of his society. His mother's house may be crowded with younger children so the warm, underground room is much more pleasant. Married men very often sleep in the kiva, too, but for different reasons. When a man marries, he goes to live with his wife in the midst of her clan relatives. Often he remains, in a sense, an outsider. While he prizes his family and his home, he prizes, also, his kiva sanctuary. When his house becomes too full of words, he can retire to the peace and quiet and good fellowship of this club room which protects him from family troubles.

A typical kiva is a circular, subterranean room, twelve to fourteen feet in diameter and seven or eight feet deep. Its walls are faced with stone to hold back the surrounding earth. At a height of about three feet from the floor the walls are stepped back so there is a ledge or shelf, at least a foot wide running entirely around the room. Resting on this ledge are six small masonry pillars, evenly spaced around the room, that support the roof. These pillars divide the space above the ledge into six recesses, the one to the south usually being deeper than the rest. The tops of the pillars are a couple of feet below the ground level and this space is built up with a cribbing of logs on which rests the roof of logs and adobe. The only door is a small hatchway in the center of the roof.

The kiva is entered by means of a ladder which rests on the floor and extends up through the small door. This door is also the smokehole for directly below it in the center of the kiva floor is a firepit. Fresh air is brought into the room through a small, vertical shaft back of the deep recess on the south side of the kiva. The top of the shaft is a small opening in the court-yard while the bottom opens into the kiva just above the floor. As the smoke and hot air rise through the doorway fresh air is drawn down the ventilator shaft. Between the ventilator opening and the firepit is a small masonry screen, or deflector, that keeps the fresh air from blowing across the fire.

On the other side of the firepit, opposite the deflector, is a small hole in the kiva floor, three or four inches in diameter and only slightly deeper. This small opening is of extreme im-portance to the priests. It is the sipapu, the symbolic entrance to the underworld. Many of the gods live in the Mother Earth and the prayers of the medicine men reach them through the small opening. The hole is merely a symbol. It represents the opening through which the Indians feel they themselves and all other living things emerged from the Earth Mother.

The people believe the Sun is their father and the Earth their mother. After the union of the two, the people and all other creatures first came into being in a dark cave in the center of the earth, the world of darkness. After a time they climbed up to another cave where there was a little light. This was the world of twilight. For a short time they lived in this twilight world, then they climbed to another cave with still more light, the world of dawn. Finally, they emerged through a small hole in the earth, Sipapu, and were in the present world. All other creatures emerged just as they did; all life came from the Mother Earth.

The little hole in the kiva floor is merely a symbolic sipapu, representing that original Sipapu through which the people emerged from the Mother Earth. It is a symbolic entrance to the spirit world below. During the ceremonies, offerings are placed in the hole or around it and the priests send their prayers through it to the gods who live in the underworld. And when a person dies, his spirit goes back through Sipapu to a pleasant afterworld within the Earth Mother.

When a ceremony is in progress, the kiva is sacred to the members of the society. Food is brought to them by the women and they eat and sleep in the kiva, leaving it only to perform ceremonial errands. Day and night they follow the sacred ritual, preparing their paraphernalia, recounting legends, chanting endless prayers, making offerings to the gods and performing the various ceremonial acts that are prescribed.

In some of the ceremonies the costumed priests emerge from the kiva and perform public dances or rituals. The villagers gather on the roofs surrounding the dance court and watch with serious reverence. They know these ceremonies are necessary if the delicate adjustment is to be maintained between the people and the mysterious powers which affect them.

At the end of the ceremony the kiva becomes a club room and workshop again. Paraphernalia is stored away on the ledges or in small niches in the kiva walls and normal life resumes. A kiva presents a varied scene, for any activity carried on by the men may be performed there. Undisturbed by outsiders they work, loaf, gamble, gossip, trade and sleep in this room which is their most prized possession. Since the women own the homes the kiva is the only bit of real property the men can call their own.

Because of the strange social and religious customs a man's life is divided into three parts. His family life centers about his wife's house for there live the wife and children whom he cherishes and for whom he provides. His social life centers about his mother's home for there lies his clan affiliation. His religious life centers in the kiva which belongs to his religious society or fraternity. These three interests do not conflict. They dovetail perfectly, each taking its proper share of the man's time and attention.

The life of a woman is much less complicated. Most of her activities concern the home and family and her full time is occupied with them.

Some of the most important religious duties of the men are concerned with a great ceremonial building which stands on the

The kiva roof formed an open court where many activities took place

Interior details of the kiva

mesa top just across the canyon from Cliff Palace. It is a massive, D-shaped building which dominates a high, narrow point between two canyons. Near it are a number of cliff dwellings and the men from all these joined in constructing the building. On days when it is used, priests and men from all the villages come trotting up the trails to join in the performance of the elaborate ceremonies. It is a superceremonial structure where only the most important rites are performed.

When the building was constructed, the priests planned it very carefully. The main building is D-shaped, with the straight wall to the south. The outside wall is double and in the space between are a number of long narrow rooms, some without doorways. In the court enclosed by the walls are two kivas. This part of the building is symmetrical, the result of the very careful planning of the priests. On the west end of the building is an addition consisting of a kiva and ten rooms, all added in such a way that the entire building is still D-shaped. The building has no roof and all of the walls are over a dozen feet high. Half of the rooms have no doors; they are deep, small rooms entered by ladders.

This building is open to the sun and the elements, in this respect being entirely different from the underground kivas. The thick, high, double walls and the location on the isolated point give the priests the secrecy they desire and in this unique building are held the greatest of all the ceremonies. Long ago the priests of the various villages decided there was a need for this community place of worship. By concerted effort they built it and through the cooperation of the many societies they have carried on the ceremonies. It is their supreme effort toward a perfect adjustment with the powers that control their destiny.

During the late fall and early winter the ceremonial season is in full swing and there is much festivity in Cliff Palace. It is a time for visiting and feasting and there is a trace of the carnival spirit in the air. The ceremonies are not entirely solemn, long-faced affairs; some have light, entertaining parts and there may even be clowns who convulse the onlookers with their antics. The underlying motive of a ceremony is serious and earnest but this does not prevent its being thoroughly enjoyable to the participants as well as the audience.

Visitors are drawn to the ceremonies from far and wide. Their strongest desire may be to see an important ceremony but even more often the strongest motive is the desire to join in the festivities that accompany it. There is always a gay crowd, much talking and visiting and an abundance of good food. When the Crier Chief announces the date for a ceremony, the news spreads rapidly and the men of other villages come flocking in. It is a grand excuse for a visit to the big city to feast, gossip, trade, and incidentally, to witness a ceremony.

Although the women play only a small part in the religious work, they are always busy during the ceremonies for they must feed the participants and the visitors. The ceremony may last for as many as nine days and large quantities of food must be prepared. The women and girls are busy over the cooking fires day after day.

The basic food article is corn in some form; it is the backbone of every meal. Corn is by far the most abundant foodstuff and through the generations the women have devised many ways of cooking it to prevent its becoming monotonous. The corn is ground by the younger women on the metates, smooth flat stones that are slanted into small bins. Under the lower end of each metate is a clean adobe basin that gathers the meal. The woman kneels at the upper end of the metate, places the corn on it, and grinds it with a smaller, flat stone, the mano, which she holds in her hands. Sliding the mano back and forth across the metate she grinds the corn until a fine meal results. This is slow back-breaking work but the women are forced to do it day after day. When a great deal of meal must be produced for a ceremonial feast, several of the women grind together. Often the young men sing for the grinders and a fast snappy tune not only cheers the women but causes the grinding stones to move much faster.

After the corn meal is prepared it can be cooked in a number of ways. The simple batter may be baked in small cakes on a hot stone. Juniper ashes may be added to make the cakes blue. The dough may be rolled in corn husks and baked in the ashes or large cakes may be baked in hot pits. If fine and coarse corn meal are mixed, rolled into little balls and boiled in a pot of stew, tasty dumplings result.

A real delicacy results when the corn bread is sweetened with saliva. In making this sweet bread a portion of the corn meal is chewed by the women until the saliva changes the starch to sugar. When this chewed meal is mixed with the rest of the meal and baked in corn husks, a sweet bread results. If the chewed batter is rolled up in fresh corn leaves and boiled, the resulting dumpling-like balls are the sweetest food known to the people. The chewed foods are real delicacies and are made especially for honored guests.

In addition to the corn dishes, there is a great variety of other foods. Meat of all kinds is roasted, boiled or stewed. Broths, soups and stews are common. Boiled beans and baked squash are always part of a feast and any of these articles may be cooked in combination. In addition there are wild plant dishes; boiled greens, boiled or baked roots, stewed fruits, roasted seeds or ground pinon nuts.

Fall is the time when there is the greatest abundance and variety of foods and the feasts that accompany the ceremonies are sumptuous affairs. The finest dishes are passed down into the kivas to the priests. Guests eat in the open courts around the cooking fires and drowsily belch their gratitude for the food and hospitality.

In the evening the people gather around the many small fires that send dancing shadows across the roof of the great cave. From some of the kivas comes the chanting of the priests; from others come the more uncertain voices of the boys as they learn the endless songs. Some of the groups around the fires are also singing but most of them are quietly talking, gambling and sleeping.

The canyon is lighted by the bright rays of a golden harvest moon and the cliffs echo the voices of the singers, not only from Cliff Palace but from all the other cliff dwellings up and down the canyons. The great green mesa is filled with happy, thankful people and troubles seem far away. The gods are pleased with the efforts of the industrious Indians.

As autumn fades into winter the people of Cliff Palace face it with confidence. Winter is always an ordeal but they are well-prepared. There is an abundance of food and there is ample clothing. Great piles of wood have been gathered and the houses have carefully been rechinked. There will be suffering and many deaths during the cold months that are ahead but spring is just beyond.

7

WINTER

Winter is the least enjoyable of all seasons for the people of Cliff Palace. It is a long, quiet, cold season, when the witches plague the people with their evil deeds. There is much sickness and suffering and often the sadness of death hangs over the town. Those who are active and healthy do not mind it so much, but it is an uncomfortable season for the children and an agonizing time for older men and women who suffer from rheumatism and arthritis.

During the late fall the weather has grown colder and colder and now in December comes true winter. Cold winds sweep down from the mountains to the north, bringing the snow: soon the mesa tops are white. In the vicinity of Cliff Palace it seldom gets deep. When it reaches a depth of a foot, it is considered heavy, but if it reaches a depth of two feet or more the people talk excitedly about it and the old men begin to recall the heavy snows of by-gone days. The snow will not remain on the ground all winter for the mesa slopes to the south and the rays of the sun beat directly down upon it. The first December snow will soon melt and the mesa tops will be dry for a time. Then another snow storm will turn it white again but that, too, will melt away and so it will continue through the winter. Occasionally, there will be warm days when the mesa tops will be muddy and small streams of water will come trickling down the cliffs.

As the cold increases the people gradually become accustomed to it. Their houses are never perfectly warm and comfortable so their strong, healthy bodies become hardened to the chill of the shadowy cave. Sometimes the night temperatures drop close to, or even below, zero. Since the cave faces west the sun does not come in until the middle of the afternoon and during the morning the temperature rises very little. When the sun finally comes into the cave in the afternoon it brings a sudden warmth and for a couple of hours the people are almost comfortable.

There are old men in the town who can remember when all of the people lived in pueblos on the mesa top and they never stop telling about those better days. The moment the sun came up in the morning the temperature began to rise and all through the day it warmed the open pueblos. The old men insist the people were happier then, the witches were less troublesome and there was less sickness. Remembering those sunny days the old men mutter about the depressing shadows that chill Cliff Palace during the winter.

Dozens of small fires burn constantly in the cave and those fires, in addition to the natural warmth of hundreds of closely crowded people, dull the sharpest edge of the cold. Clothing is the final defense and as the severity of winter increases, more and more is worn.

Cotton cloth, feather blankets and buckskin robes are worn in every conceivable manner except as actual tailored garments. The nearest approach to tailored clothing is an occasional slip-over buckskin jacket without sleeves. Sometimes a robe is slit in the center and slipped, poncho-like, over the head. Pieces of feather cloth, cotton cloth or buckskin are tied about the body as close-fitting jackets or draped, skirt-like, from the waist. Large, soft feather blankets and buckskin robes are draped over the shoulders and drawn in about the body. Short leggins are made of buckskin, or woven of human hair, to add to the comfort of the lower legs.

Taken as a whole, they are a raggedy-looking crowd but the clothing does give protection against the cold. The people have tanned buckskin in abundance, there is considerable cotton cloth and each person has at least one feather robe. By utilizing these in every possible way the desired effect is achieved, even though neat tailoring is unknown.

Shadowy though the cave may be, it is free of wind and snow and while complete comfort may seldom be attained, except in the kivas, most of the people become accustomed to the chill. But those who are naturally weak and those who are weakened by illness or age suffer greatly from the cold of winter.

There is less activity than during any other season. When the mesas are fairly clear of snow the men often go after firewood and they always keep enough on hand to last through a long period of deep snow. When the people first moved into the cave, firewood was close at hand. The slope in front of the cave was covered with pinon and juniper trees and the mesa top above the cave was heavily forested. But now, after generations of use, there are no trees left near the town and the men must go far across the mesa top for firewood. This is a problem that always faces the people for during the winter vast amounts of wood are used. Sometimes villages must be deserted because of the failure of the supply of firewood.

When the men bring the wood in from the mesa, they carry it to the top of the cliff at either end of the cave. After shouting to make sure no one is below, they hurl the logs over the cliff to crash on the rocks below. The shattering crash saves much chopping with stone axes and the women gather the splintered pieces and store them in the cave.

Winter is a good season for hunting and when the snows are not too deep the young men often go out in search of deer and mountain sheep. Deep snows on the high northern rim of the mesa have forced the animals down to the lower parts and the men do not have far to go for their game.

When they are not busy gathering wood and hunting, the men spend most of their time in the kivas. They have a decided advantage over the women and children in this one respect for the kivas are completely comfortable. Being entirely underground, and with only the one small door in the roof, a kiva is kept perfectly warm by a small fire in the central firepit. Fresh air comes down the ventilator shaft to drive the smoke out through the door and the lower part of the room is never smoky. The floor is covered with mats and skins and the men loaf, sleep and work in perfect comfort. Unmarried boys who have been initiated into the religious societies live in the kivas most of the time during the winter and the married men often sleep in them. They are far more comfortable than the houses.

Women and children, having few kiva privileges, are forced to spend their time in the courts, where they huddle around the fires, and in the houses. Few of the houses have fires inside for in the small, unventilated rooms the smoke is almost unbearable. Sometimes an older person prefers the discomfort of smoke to the misery of the cold and a fire is built in a house. A smoky, soot-blackened room results.

At night the women and children snuggle close together for warmth. The floor of the house is covered with skins, blankets and heavy mats woven of reeds, juniper bark or yucca fibers. Sometimes deep, soft layers of corn shucks and tassels are spread on the floor and the blankets are spread on them. The last person into the room reaches back out through the door, picks up the thin sandstone door slab that is leaning against the wall, and fits it carefully into the opening. With the soft floor coverings and plenty of warm blankets and skins the closely-snuggled women and children spend the cold nights in comparative comfort.

During the warmer seasons the people arose at dawn but now they stay in bed until a much later hour. Actually they are more comfortable in their beds and since there is no important work to be done, there is no need for early rising.

As soon as the women stir out of their blankets, they start the fires and when there is sufficient warmth the children crawl out to huddle about the flames. On each fire a large jar of water is heating and when it finally boils a special corn meal, which was made from fresh corn at harvest time, is stirred in. This makes a thin corn gruel and mugs of the nourishing hot drink are passed to the waiting children. By mid-morning the breakfast of corn bread and meat is ready and the men, most of whom have spent the night in the kiva, join their families around the fires. Late in the afternoon the second meal of the day is served and it is always more elaborate; meat, corn bread, beans, and squash in various combinations, seasoned with dried fruits, roots and berries which were gathered in abundance during the fall. Food is a most important factor in the fight against the rigors of winter and the women spend long hours around the cooking fires.

There is no water problem during the winter. Ice and snow are brought in and melted and springs which have a southern exposure continue to flow. Less water is needed than at any other season so the women spend very little time obtaining the necessary supplies. Most of their time is occupied with corn grinding, cooking, and the care of the smaller children. Occasionally a woman weaves a basket but pottery is seldom made during the cold season. Principally, the women are occupied with keeping their families warm and well fed.

For the men, winter is an easy time. Once in a while they leave the cave to go hunting and wood gathering or to trot off to another village to gamble or witness a ceremony but for the most part they seldom stray far from their warm, comfortable kivas. There they work leisurely at their various crafts, producing the many things they need. Winter is a fine time for weaving since it can be done in the kiva. Many ceremonies are performed during the winter months, not only the regular ceremonies which are performed at exactly the same time each year, but countless healing ceremonies which are conducted whenever there is sickness in the town. Winter is also a fine time for training the boys in ceremonial ways and there is much story-telling, singing and chanting as the boys broaden their religious background.

In the early winter one important ceremony is held when the priests "turn back the sun." Every day since early summer the sun has moved farther and farther south along the western horizon. At last, in late December, he has reached the point beyond which he must not be allowed to go. The priests know the spot well: it is on the horizon directly over a certain mark on the opposite canyon wall. When the sun reaches this spot each year the priests perform the ceremony that causes him to cease his southern journey and start back to the north again. If the priests fail to please the Sun Father, or if he is angry with the people, he will continue his journey to the south and perpetual cold and darkness will envelope the earth. Never yet have the priests failed; always the sun has been pleased and after reaching that certain spot he has reversed and started back to the north to bring the long days and the warmth of summer.

When the Sun Watcher finds that the setting sun has reached the proper spot, the Crier Chief makes the announcement and the priests begin their ceremony. Day after day it continues until they see that the sun has started back to the north. There is great rejoicing in Cliff Palace: the sun has heeded the prayers and is coming back. The happy people marvel at the power of their priests who have never failed in this important duty.

As winter progresses and the cold increases, witches become more and more active and there is much sickness in the town. Throughout the winter the medicine men and the medicine societies are busy in their efforts to counteract the evil powers of the witches who cause all serious diseases. Minor ailments, which the people can understand, are not considered to result from witchcraft. If a person gets a grain of sand in his eye, if a child gets a bone caught in its throat, or if a child has a sudden stomach-ache from overeating, it is considered to be the natural result of something the people can see and understand. But the serious illnesses, which strike so mysteriously, are not natural and are considered to result from the evil practices of witches. Only the medicine men, with their supernatural powers, can combat the witch-caused diseases and the medicine men and the medicine societies are busy with their healing ceremonies. During the winter witches always seem to be more active and as a result there is more sickness and death than at other times. The people are often uneasy and there is not the happiness which was so prevalent during the other seasons. It is not simply because there is sickness and suffering – it is more because of the fear which is in the hearts of the people. Any person may be a witch and usually it is impossible to tell who is causing the trouble.

Children suffer a great deal and all through the winter they sniffle and cough with colds. Sometimes the colds settle in the sinuses, in the ears or even in the lungs, bringing complications against which the priests are powerless. Often the end is slow in coming. When a cold settles in the middle ear and an abscessed mastoid results, the terrible agony may last for weeks before the inevitable result brings an end to the suffering. Sometimes the end comes quickly and a mother hardly realizes that her baby is sick before it is gone.

Many of the older people are suffering from the agony of decayed and abscessed teeth. All their lives they have been eating the gritty corn bread that has come from the soft grinding stones. As a result, their teeth are badly ground away; sometimes they are ground down to the gums. With the loss of the tooth enamel, decay has come and now aching and abscessed teeth are the result. Here is an old fellow with a great cavity in each molar; half of them are throbbing with pain as the cold air hits the exposed nerves. Here is an old man suffering the agony of three abscessed upper teeth; at night he walks the floor moaning with pain. This old fellow's lower right canine tooth developed a cystoid abscess; it has eaten through his cheek causing an ugly running sore on his face. In one house is an old woman who long ago lost all her teeth; years of chewing on her gums have caused them to recede until now her nose and chin almost touch. Yonder is an old man who for months has had an aching molar. In order to ease the pain he has been chewing on the other side and now those teeth are so badly ground away that they too are aching. So it is throughout the city. Decayed, abscessed and impacted teeth, pyorrhea and other dental ailments are common.

The medicine men have little success in their efforts to combat the agony of an aching or abscessed tooth. Finally, if the patient can no longer bear the pain, the tooth is extracted and in this the suffering person has two choices. One method is to knock the tooth out. One end of a piece of bone or hard wood is placed against the base of the tooth and an obliging neighbor taps the other end sharply with a stone axe. Instantly the tooth is gone! The other method of extraction is equally simple. A long, strong piece of sinew is obtained and one end is tied securely around the aching tooth. The other end of the sinew is tied to a large rock. Then the rock is thrown away. And with it goes the tooth!

If the patient is unable to face the drastic extraction, the tooth is simply allowed to abscess and slough away. Sometimes an aged person loses every tooth in this manner. One after another they abscess and slough out until at last the helpless victim is able to relax in the blessed state of painless toothlessness.

Many of the people, especially the older ones, are suffering from rheumatism and arthritis. There are many specific causes but often it is merely the breakdown that comes from a life of exposure and hard work. The people age early and although there are a few very old men and women in the town the average life expectancy is low. Before middle age is reached many are unable to bear their share of the work. Limbs are swollen and stiffened with arthritis and rheumatism, and spines are stiffened or even partially or completely solidified with arthritis. When these conditions come, the bent and crippled oldsters seldom venture far from the cave. They are cared for and honored by their children and their clan relatives.

In addition to the many diseases that afflict the people, there are often injuries. During the winter, snow and ice gather in the toe-holds on the cliffs and climbers, becoming momentarily careless, sometimes crash on the rocks below. Fractured skulls, arms and legs result and their treatment gives the priests some of their most serious problems. Compound fractures result in fatal infections and the medicine men can do little in the case of a serious fracture of the skull. Simple fractures of the lower arm or leg are often treated successfully. Thin splints of wood are bound to the limb to hold the bones in position and after the break has healed, full use of the member is often regained. A fracture of the upper arm or leg is seldom treated with success for the powerful muscles pull the bones out of the position and, if the victim survives, a crippled limb results. Over in the north end of the town lives a young lady of nineteen who suffered an accident of this type. Returning from the spring one day with a heavy jar of water on her head, she missed her step and fell over a low cliff. Her left femur was broken just below the hip. Instead of knitting properly, the broken ends of the bone slipped past each other and grew together side by side, with a two inch overlap. The young lady is able to hobble about with the aid of a crutch but her left leg is two inches shorter than the right.

The medicine men wage a constant battle against the diseases and injuries which afflict the people. Against some of the diseases they have little success: it simply means that the witches who are to blame are too strong. In other cases the medicine man wins and the patient recovers. Ailments which originate in the mind are common and are easily cured. Since the people live in constant fear of witches, they often feel they have been bewitched by some evil person. This causes them to imagine strange ailments and the medicine men are called upon to counteract the evil spell. Such ailments are easily treated for the patient's faith in the medicine man and the constant promise of a cure soon drive away the imagined troubles.

When a person becomes ill, a family council is held and it is decided that a medicine man, or doctor, must be called. The father, or some male relative, mixes a small amount of corn meal with powdered turquoise and wraps it in a corn husk. This he takes to the medicine man and, placing it in his hand, tells him what is wanted. The medicine man agrees to come in the evening. During the day the family prepares food, while the doctor prays and prepares his medicines. In the evening the doctor comes to the patient's home and prepares for the examination. Smearing ashes on his hands, as protection against witches, he removes the patient's clothing and feels over his body, searching for the cause of the illness. Upon completing his diagnosis, the doctor mixes a medicine of powdered herbs and water and gives it to the patient to drink. Then, after assuring the patient that he will recover, the doctor leaves.

If, however, the patient fails to recover and grows worse, the entire medicine society is called in. Again, the father takes corn meal and powdered turquoise to the medicine man and requests that the society perform a healing ceremony. If the patient's condition is critical, the doctor agrees to bring the members of the society in the evening. If there seems to be no immediate emergency, he agrees to bring them after four days have passed.

During the four-day period, preparations are made. The priests pray and get their ceremonial equipment ready and each morning, in order to cleanse themselves, drink emetics that cause them to vomit. The family of the sick person prepares great quantities of food so the priests may be fed and all members of the family cleanse themselves by vomiting each morning. If the emetic does not cause vomiting, a long feather is thrust down the person's throat until the desired result is obtained.

On the evening of the fourth day the patient is taken into the kiva of the medicine society. Two men, armed with bows and arrows, are stationed outside the kiva to keep witches away. On the kiva floor the priests have made a small painting by using corn meal of different colors and around the painting are prayersticks, fetishes of the curing animals, rattles, eagle feathers, bags of herb medicines and other ceremonial equipment. Upon entering the kiva, the patient sits down or, if he is very ill, lies down in front of the meal-painting.

The doctors, faces painted and wearing only their loincloths, are seated behind the painting. They are singing and the songs, which continue for some time, are an effort to induce the spirits of the curing animals, the mountain lion, bear, badger, wolf, eagle and shrew to enter the kiva. These animals have great supernatural healing powers and their spirits must be present in the kiva. As the singing continues, two doctors step out and do a short dance, then another doctor comes forward to prepare the medicine. Stirring some of the powdered herbs into a bowl of water, he ladles it out to the patient and all other persons in the kiva.

Now it is time for the most important part of the ceremony: they must find the object which is causing the disease. One of the doctors rubs ashes on his hands and begins to search the patient's body for the object which a witch has shot into it. After careful search, he locates the object and sucks it out of the patient's body. Spitting the object into his hand, he shows it to everyone. It is a centipede!

The doctors have also found that the patient's heart has been stolen by witches and now they must get it back. Two of the doctors smear themselves with ashes and, with stone knives in their hands, climb out of the kiva. Soon the people hear sounds of fighting down on the trash pile in front of the cave. There are loud cries and the sounds of struggling, and blows being struck. Then all is quiet and other doctors go out to bring the two back. One of the doctors is unconscious and must be carried into the kiva and both show the marks of a furious struggle. But they have recovered the patient's heart – it is a little ball of rags. When the ball is cut open, a grain of corn is found in the center and this is given to the patient to swallow. Now that he has recovered his heart he will soon be well.

The ceremony is over and as the patient returns to his home the doctors put away their ceremonial equipment. Soon the women of the patient's family bring food which they have prepared and the medicine men have a fine feast. Baskets of cornmeal are also brought to the medicine men in payment for the cure which they have effected.

At any time of the year there may be sickness in Cliff Palace but there is always the greatest amount in the winter. Seldom during the cold season are the people entirely free from it. The medicine men carry out the prescribed ceremonies, sometimes succeeding, sometimes failing. When they effect a cure there is rejoicing but when they fail there is sadness in the city and the relatives of the unfortunate person are plunged into mourning.

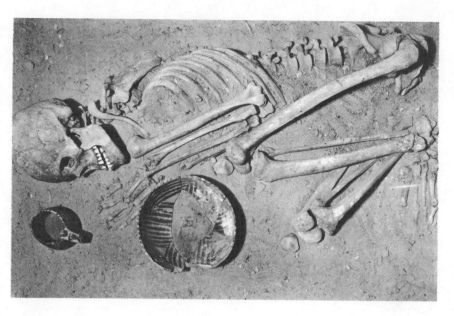

Bodies were usually buried in a folded position

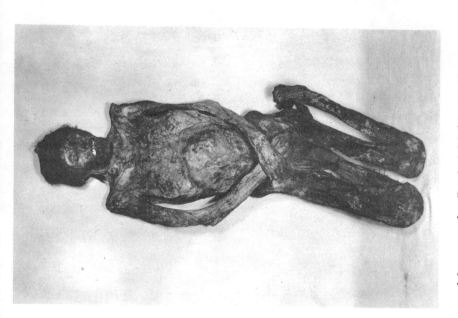

Mummy of a Basket Maker woman

Very soon after death comes preparations are made for the burial. The body is bathed and the hair is washed. The arms are folded across the chest and tied together to hold them in position. The legs are folded up against the body. Around the tightly-flexed body is wrapped a cotton blanket, then a large feather blanket. Finally the bundle is wrapped in a piece of matting and is ready for burial.

There is no cemetery and the burial may be made anywhere. When the weather is good the bodies may be buried out on the mesa top or anywhere in the canyon. Sometimes they are placed in crevices in the cliffs or in holes under large boulders. During the winter, when the ground is frozen and covered with snow, graves are often dug in the great trash pile in front of the cave. For generations the people have dumped their ashes and refuse there and it is not difficult to dig a grave in the soft, ashy material.

Occasionally death comes when a severe storm is raging outside the cave. Rather than face the storm the men of a burial party sometimes seal a body in an empty house or bury it in the trash room in the rear of the cave. The cave roof is too low for houses in that space so the long, low room is used as a trash room and turkey roost. When a body is buried there it is surrounded by perfectly dry materials such as ashes, dust, corn cobs, corn tassels and turkey droppings. The chill of winter prevents decay and the body begins to dry out. Soon all moisture is gone and only the bones and dried tissues remain. If no moisture reaches it, the dry, mummy-like body will remain unchanged for centuries.

After the grave is dug the tightly-wrapped body is placed in it. Food and water are placed in the grave, along with the personal possessions of the deceased; weapons, tools, jewelry and other articles which the spirit of the dead person will need in the afterworld. After the grave is filled with earth and rocks the members of the burial party return to their homes and purify themselves by washing their hair, vomiting and fumigating their clothing in smoke.

The spirit of the deceased does not leave the body for four days so each morning relatives place food and water on the grave. At sunrise on the fourth morning the spirit leaves the body and journeys back through Sipapu, into the Mother Earth, where the dead live in another world much like this one. As soon as the spirit is gone the relatives purify themselves and from this time on try not to speak of, or think of the dead person again. Grieving may cause sickness so the dead are best forgotten.

The winter passes slowly. For those who are strong and active it has no terrors although it may cause a certain amount of discomfort. For those who are weak and sick it becomes an ordeal. At no time during the winter is Cliff Palace free from sickness and suffering and the spirits of the people are often low. In January the cold becomes more intense. Scores of fires burn brightly in the great cave as the people attempt to drive out the cold. Some nights the temperature falls very close to zero. High overhead hangs a brilliant white moon and the snowy canyon is almost as light as day. From the cliff near the great ceremonial building comes the wail of a coyote: from the mesa top comes the mournful hoot of an owl. The cave is quiet except for low chanting in some of the kivas and the snoring of old men. Sometimes a baby whimpers or a sick person groans. Now and then a muffled scream echoes through the cave as an aged sufferer cries out from the agony of arthritis or an abscessed tooth.

There is little travel during the coldest periods. The men forego their hunting and visiting and everyone stays close to the sheltering cave with the single idea of keeping warm and well. The city is quieter now: there is none of the boisterous gaiety that was so pronounced during the other seasons.

The men spend most of their time in the kivas while the women and children gather around the fires in the courtyards. The turkeys roost in the back of the cave at night and come out in the daytime to wander about the courts and roof-tops and fight with the dogs for scraps of food that are thrown to them. During periods when there is deep snow in the canyon, the turkeys are fed small amounts of the precious corn but in late winter they grow thin and bedraggled. When they are not roaming about the city searching for food they sit in quiet rows on the housetops, feathers fluffed against the cold. The turkeys are highly prized, both for their meat and for their feathers, but they lead a miserable existence. They do not thrive in the cold shadowy cave and the flocks usually are not large. Not only are they tormented by children and dogs but regularly they suffer the indignity of having their feathers plucked for use in ceremonies and in the manufacture of feather blankets.

As the end of winter draws near the food becomes more monotonous. Many of the tastier foods are gone: the supplies of pinon nuts, dried fruits, roots, squash and dried berries are completely exhausted. Now each meal consists of meat, corn bread and beans. Sometimes the meat is fresh but usually it is meat that was dried last fall. This meat is as hard as rawhide and must be pounded with stones and thoroughly cooked before it can be eaten. In order to gain variety the women bake the corn bread in every possible way and corn meal, meat and beans are combined in numerous forms. Still the food is monotonous and everyone longs for something green.

In February the snows become heavy and wet and in the latter part of the month there is rain. Even though the rain does not come into the cave everything becomes damp. The days are getting warmer now and as a result a foul odor hangs over the city.

At any time of the year a strong odor of decaying animal and vegetable matter and human offal fills the cave. Out in front is the great trash pile and in the rear is the trash room where the turkeys roost and where some of the dead are buried. In addition to this, the people have no idea of personal sanitation. In the warmer seasons they usually step outside the cave but in the winter they merely step back into the turkey roost or out on the front terraces.

Because of this there is always a heavy odor about the city. In the summer it is not so bad for the women often sweep out the houses and courts and throw the trash out in front of the cave where the hot sun drys out the waste materials. In the winter there is less of this cleaning and the trash and filth accumulate. The dampness in the air causes mould and mustiness and when the warm wet days of late winter come the air is foul with the odor of decaying matter.

The people do not notice this odor. Their first breath of life was like that and they merely think it is the way air smells.

As the end of winter draws near the cold grows less intense. There are still occasional snowstorms but they are warm and wet and melt rapidly. The mesas are soggy with mud and small streams of water trickle over the cliffs as the snow disappears. The air is warm and balmy: during the middle of the day it is often hot. Grass turns green in the sheltered spots and the buds on the shrubs begin to swell. Chipmunks and squirrels come out of hibernation to greet the spring.

The people of Cliff Palace have been noting all of these signs and there is a stir of activity in the city as they throw off the cloak of winter. It was this promise of spring that helped them through. Sometimes they have been cold and there has been sickness and death. At times there has been a heavy pall of sadness over the city. Now all that is over for spring is in the air.

The people are happy and smiling as they bustle about preparing for the work that is ahead. The men think of their farms, the women think of making pottery, repairing and building houses, and arranging marriages. The children, turkeys and dogs think of nothing: they merely dash out of the shadowy cave into the warm spring sunshine.

Our year with the people of Cliff Palace has ended. Spring, summer, autumn and winter have passed. Now spring has arrived to start the eternal cycle all over again.

8

THE END OF THE STORY

The year we have just spent with the people of Cliff Palace was a normal year for all of the people of the Mesa Verde. We have seen the daily events in one cliff dwelling and we may feel sure that similar events were taking place in each of the many hundreds of cliff dwellings on the great mesa.

There was not a single occurrence that made it any different from the countless other normal years they experienced. It did not remain long in their memories for it was just one more year when all of the forces of nature worked in perfect harmony. There was an abundance of snow and rain, and food was plentiful. There were no catastrophies or memorable events.

Good years, such as that one, were soon forgotten. The years they remembered were those that brought sadness or disaster. Talkative old men long remembered the years of terrific drouth or the year the crops were destroyed by forest fires. They did not soon forget the evil summer when almost all of the babies died of a strange malady, and for centuries the storytellers recalled the year when a monster swallowed the sun completely for a few minutes. Those were the unusual years and they served as mile posts. Time was measured from them.

The years of catastrophe did not come often. It was only occasionally that the crops failed and when they did the people were prepared for it. A thousand years of farming in the Mesa Verde had taught them that every few years they must expect a dry year without a harvest. Often they were able to predict such a season in advance. If the heavy snows of December and January and February failed to come, the men began to worry. Then if the spring rains failed to come, the farmers became quite sure that the harvests would be poor. Months in advance they began to prepare for the lean year that faced them.

Food was measured out sparingly: not a grain of corn or a pinch of meal was wasted. The women searched endlessly for wild plant foods and the men went hunting day after day. By living more on meat and wild plants they were able to conserve the stores of corn and beans. Water supplies were built up and they tried to enter the summer season with every available drop stored in their jars and in the pools in the canyon. New springs were developed and in extreme cases the women even walked four miles down the canyon to the Mancos River for water.

By skillfully adjusting themselves to conditions the people were able to survive a year of drouth with little difficulty. A second year of crop failure was very serious but still it could be managed and occasionally during their occupancy of the Mesa Verde they had even survived periods of drouth that lasted several years. Such an ordeal brought suffering and hardship: it meant death for many of the weaker people. But still it could be endured.

So it was that when drouth settled down upon the Mesa Verde in the year 1276 A.D., the people thought nothing of it. They had just enjoyed several good years and they worried little when the crops failed. They took the usual precautions and the priests assured them that the next year would be normal again. But the drouth did not break. Year after year it continued. A generation passed and still the drouth did not end.

The rings of trees which grew at that time show that the drouth continued for twenty-four years. From 1276, through 1299, rainfall was below normal in the Mesa Verde and sur- rounding regions. Many of the years were unbelievably dry. Some were only moderately dry and a few were almost normal. But throughout the long period, rainfall was far below average. Winter snows were light and failed to restore the soil moisture. Summer rains were often completely lacking. Each year the soil lost more of its moisture and only the hardiest plants were able to survive. During the entire period there probably was not a harvest worthy of the name.

The drouth was the worst ever known in the Southwest and its effect on the people of the Mesa Verde was tragic. Year after year the crops withered in the fields. Wild food plants also died or failed to reproduce. The larger game animals drifted off to the mountains and the smaller animals dimished in numbers. In their search for food the women scoured the mesas until there was not an edible plant left. The men hunted far and wide with less and less luck. Still the drouth continued. Water supplies dwindled. During the winter the pools in the canyon failed to fill and the lack of moisture caused the springs to become mere trickles. It was impossible to wring water from the earth when no water was there.

The people were faced with three terrors; the lack of food, the lack of water, and the wrath of the gods. The first two actually existed; the last existed only in their minds. Consequently, it was the worst of all. Added to their tragic need of food and water was the horrible fear that their gods had deserted them.

How the priests must have labored. Every ceremony, every trick they knew was repeated time after time as the drouth progressed. The cliff dwellings echoed with the chants and Sun Temple, the great ceremonial building, must have been the scene of countless super-ceremonials as the priests of the various villages threw their combined strength into the fight.

Still the drouth continued!

Throughout the Mesa Verde there was much death from starvation and disease. Food and water were practically exhausted. The tragic moment came when they were forced to eat the seed corn. This was the last resort: it could be fatal to farmers. Only when death faced them did they sacrifice the precious seed for there could never be another crop unless they were fortunate enough to find other people with surplus supplies. The result was inevitable. Since the drouth would not end the people could only drift away, hoping to find better conditions elsewhere. It was their only chance of survival.

The migration from the Mesa Verde must have taken place gradually. As a matter of fact, there are indications that the migrations began even before the drouth came. At an earlier date vast areas around the Mesa Verde were occupied by members of the same tribe. Some time before 1200 A.D., however, the population began to dwindle and by the time the drouth came almost all of the area, except the Mesa Verde, was deserted.

In all probability, these early migrations were caused by pressure from an enemy tribe for there is much to indicate that

the people were in trouble. Certainly the population was dwindling long before the great drouth began. The identity of the
enemy is not definitely known. It has been suggested that the
Apaches may have entered the region at that time, or possibly
the early Utes. No definite evidence of the enemy people has
been found but their pressure is indicated by their effect upon
the peaceful farming Indians.

The migration from the Mesa Verde probably took place
gradually; certainly there was no mass movement. As the
drouth continued small groups drifted off in search of better
conditions. All of the people of a small village may have moved
together but the larger towns must have broken up gradually.
Cliff Palace and other large cliff dwellings probably were deserted a clan at a time. As conditions became more desperate
the people quarreled over the dwindling supplies. There must
have been many cases of actual violence as frenzied men sought
to obtain food and water for their starving families. Dissatis-
faction and discontent mounted rapidly and the once happy towns
were abandoned by their people as clan after clan took to the
trail in search of new homes.

Before the twenty-four year drouth was over, the Mesa
Verde was entirely deserted and there is no evidence that any
of the people ever returned. Since that tragic time the cliff
dwellings have been empty and silent as they have fought against
the heavy, leveling hand of time.

When the people left the Mesa Verde their troubles were not
over. The drouth was felt all over the Southwest and life was
possible only in the most favorable spots. Added to the misfortunes of the drifting people was the increased activity of the
nomadic Indians for they, too, suffered from the drouth. It is
possible that their increased activities hastened the flight from
the Mesa Verde for they must have preyed upon the farming
peoples during the troubled times.

Although large numbers perished before and during the migration, many of the Mesa Verde Indians did survive. The major migration seems to have been to the southeast and finally
the people settled in the Rio Grande Valley. One group crossed
the river and for a time lived in the Gallisteo Basin, a short
distance southeast of the present city of Santa Fe, New Mexico.
After a time this area was deserted and the people mingled

with other Pueblo Indians along the Rio Grande. As they merged with the others they gradually lost their identity as Mesa Verde people.

During the great drouth the population of the Southwest was diminished and many regions were abandoned forever by the Pueblo Indians. When the drouth finally ended the survivors were concentrated in the most favorable spots where there were the best supplies of water, the finest farming lands or good natural defenses against the nomadic Indians.

In some regions they prospered for a time but never again did they reach the high level they had attained before the great drouth. Perhaps the drouth caused a dry rot to set in and the fortunes of the Pubelo people waned. When Coronado came there were less than eighty pueblos: today there are less than thirty.

The people of these present-day pueblos are the descendants of scores of thousands of Pueblo Indians who once lived in the Southwest. In their veins, greatly thinned by the centuries, flows the blood of the ancient people of the Mesa Verde.

PART TWO

The Archeological Background

9

ORIGIN OF THE AMERICAN INDIAN

The story of the Mesa Verde really had its beginning many thousands of years ago in a distant land. It began when the first ancient Asiatic stepped across from Siberia and became the First American. Who he was and exactly when it happened we shall never know, but it was the important first step in a long chain of events which led to the occupation of the Mesa Verde by Pueblo Indians.

There seems to be little doubt that the early inhabitants of North and South America came from Asia by that northern route. It is the only route by which men, traveling without artificial means of transportation, could have reached these western continents. Not a single insurmountable barrier, not a single impossibility lay in the path of those ancient men as they drifted with the line of least resistance. From the northwest, America was discovered and populated.

Men first came into being somewhere in the Old World. From this point of beginning they spread slowly over the face of the earth. In all directions the ancient men traveled, always on foot, always without a goal. After a time Europe, Africa and Asia were populated, but the Americas remained without men. Surrounded by vast areas of water, except at one point, the Americas were the last great land bodies to be discovered.

Finally, the day of discovery arrived. For countless centuries groups of men had been drifting over the great continent of Asia. Farther and farther they traveled until at last a group, perhaps forced on by stronger groups behind, stood on the utmost tip of northeastern Asia, the tip of Siberia now known as the East Cape.

Standing on the ocean shore those men shaded their eyes and looked out across the water. There, only fifty-six miles away, lay another land. Curiosity, or perhaps the force of "enemy pressure", urged them on. A means of crossing those fifty-six tantalizing miles was found. At last the first human foot touched American soil.

At first glance it may seem that the crossing would be impossible for men who were without boats. Such was not the case. In winter the Bering Sea often freezes over completely. Present-day Eskimos cross on the ice and only a few years ago a white man made the crossing with a dog team. Thus, primitive man needed only the winter ice in order to satisfy his curiosity about the land across the water. The journey was made even less hazardous by two islands, the Diomedes, that raised their heads in the center of the Bering Sea, cutting the crossing into two shorter jumps.

It is even possible that when those men reached that tip of Asia no water separated them from America. A strip of land may have connected the two continents. It is known very definitely that at some not far distant date the two continents were connected by land, for some of our well-known animals have crossed from one to the other. The horse and the camel developed in America and walked off to Asia. The mammoth and the bison reversed the direction and crossed from Asia to America. In order for those beasts to make the crossing, a land bridge was necessary.

When the land bridge disappeared is not known. When the first men came is not known. Certain it is, however, that if the land bridge was in existence when the first men came to America, it afforded them an easy approach. If, on the other hand, it had disappeared beneath the waves of the Bering Sea, the men must have crossed on the ice. No one can as yet be positive as to the exact manner of the crossing. The important point is that the crossing was made and America was discovered and populated. Primitive man, after hundreds of thousands of years of wandering over the Old World, had at last found the one point at which he could enter a new land.

That this new land was superior to the old soon became apparent to the newcomers. Summers were longer: winters were less severe. Hunting and fishing were excellent and in the summer edible plants were common. Truly, here was a better land.

The first crossing from Asia to America was made many thousands of years ago. From the evidence now at hand, fifteen or twenty thousand years seems to be not too great an antiquity for those first Americans. Even at that early date, however, man was well-developed mentally and physically and had all the capabilities of modern man. The first American was no primitive brute. He was Homo sapiens, little different from the fifteenth century foreigners who rediscovered America thousands of years later and gradually edged it away from its first settlers.

Primitive human remains, such as those which have been found in the Old World, have never been found in America. Man went through his developmental stages in the Old World and came to America at a late date, a fully developed human being. Pithecanthropus erectus, Sinanthropus, Homo neanderthalensis — America has never known those tongue-twisting lowbrows!

After the first discovery of the new land there were innumerable rediscoveries. One group of men after another came to America and those migrations continued for thousands of years. The latest migrants came to America very recently. Thus, America was populated by many successive waves of migration over a long period of time.

It seems, almost, that after the first group came, word may have spread from one small tribe to another that off to the east lay a better land. People were disappearing over the eastern horizon. What lay in that direction? Curiosity urged them on!

It is altogether possible that actual word of the new land in the east went back to the Asiatic continent. Perhaps there were small counter migrations or perhaps some small traveling group, feeling a bond with some other group in the old country, sent runners back to beckon them on.

Certain it is that there was not just a single migration. Numerous groups of men filtered into America over a period of thousands of years. Slowly, aimlessly, they wandered. One group pushed another and was in turn pushed by an oncoming tribe. After a time, North and South America were covered with hundreds of small tribes of Indians.

The members of these various tribes were not all alike. They differed greatly in appearance, in language, in religion and in mode of living. The answer is apparent. The various groups came from different parts of Asia. They came at different times. They settled in different parts of the New World and developed in different ways according to the natural resources in each region. As a result there came into being the many tribes of

American Indians which were in America when Columbus came on his journey of rediscovery from the east.

The early part of the story of the Americas is still hazy. In spite of many years of search by dozens of top-flight archeologists there are many unanswered questions. Each year expeditions sift through the dust of the ages on the trail of those early Americans. More often than not the trail leads to a blank wall. The ancient past of the Indian is clouded with uncertainty but the lure of the unknown still beckons to those who are endeavoring to trail him back to his Asiatic birthplace.

The great trouble is that for thousands of years the Indians lived a hunting life. They wandered from day to day, living on the natural foods they found in each day's journey. There was no permanent home, no settled life. The hunter was ever on the trail of his next meal.

Consider the life of the primitive hunter. Each morning he is awakened by the pangs of hunger in his empty, flapping paunch and he views with dismay his breakfast which is disappearing over the horizon on four strong, swift legs. Rubbing the sleep from his eyes he starts out in pursuit of his breakfast. Failing to catch up with it, he starts after his lunch. If it eludes him, he begins to work on the next meal — and the next and the next. Always he is one jump behind his food supply. When he makes a kill he gorges and smoothes the wrinkles out of his belly. When he fails, he goes hungry.

Being forced to follow the game he is ever on the move. He can have no permanent home, no pottery, nothing that cannot easily be transported on the trail. One night he sleeps under a tree and leaves behind a broken stone knife. The next night he sleeps in a cave ten miles away and discards a worn-out sandal. The third night he builds his campfire beside a lake across the mountain. On and on through the days he moves and finally, when the end comes, the animals of the wild clean and scatter his bones and they return to the dust from whence they came.

The archeologist may find the stone knife and the discarded sandal. He may even find the long-cold ashes of the campfire. But there is nothing to indicate that all three belonged to the same man. There is not a single bit of evidence that ties them together.

Thus it is with the hunter. His trail is cold: the clews are few. He is the will-o-the-wisp of the human race. He has put many gray hairs in the head of the archeologist.

All of the early inhabitants of North and South America lived a wandering, hunting life. For thousands of years they lived on the chance products, animal and plant, that nature offered. They seldom stayed long in one place: they never built a permanent thing. To date the story of the first ten or fifteen thousand years is far from complete. It can be summed up in a few words.

The men themselves have, for the most part, eluded us. The fact that they lived a wandering life and seldom, if ever, buried the dead, has made it difficult to find the bones of the men them- selves. However, the tools and weapons made and used by those men have been found in great numbers. And best of all, they have been found in situations which clearly indicate the antiquity of man in America.

A few thousand years ago there were elephants in America. The mammoth was here as well as his terrifying near-relative, the mastodon. There were horses in various parts of the country and a strange, lumbering animal, the ground sloth, was common. Tremendous bison with long sweeping horns wallowed in the bogs and camels roamed the plains.

Modern man has never seen those animals in America. They were gone long before he came. They had been extinct thousands of years before the first Europeans poked their tardy noses into the New World.

In spite of this we know that the early Indians did see them. They hunted them and lived on their flesh. They may have been a contributing factor in the extinction of some of those ancient species. Changing weather conditions thinned out the great herds and man, not yet conservation conscious, may have helped to wipe out the survivors.

How do we know?

In a number of places the implements of those early men have been found in direct association with the bones of the extinct ani- mals. The inference is unquestionable. Dart points, knives, scrapers and other implements have been found so definitely associated with the bones of animals that there can be no doubt that man and the animals existed at the same time. If those animals have been extinct for thousands of years it dates the earliest men fairly well.

One of the most important finds was made in northeastern New Mexico, near the little town of Folsom. This find was important because it was here for the first time that modern scientists were forced to admit that man had been in America a long, long time. It is also important because it has given a name to some of the ancient men. Folsom Man, the most elusive American we have yet been unable to find.

The discovery of the earliest evidences of Folsom Man is one of the strangest stories in American archeology. The events in the story covered a period of twenty-five years and it was only by chance that the important archeological evidence came to the attention of the scientific world.

Back about 1900, a negro cowboy known as Nigger George, was riding the range on the Crowfoot Ranch near the little town of Folsom, New Mexico, searching for cattle. As George rode along, he came to a deep arroyo so he turned his horse and rode along its bank. Suddenly, in the opposite wall of the arroyo, the cowboy noticed some huge bones. They were larger than any bones he had ever seen and the fact that they were washing out of the arroyo wall several feet below the surface was puzzling. Fortunately George, although an illiterate man, was curious about the bones and, instead of riding on and forgetting them, collected a number and took them to the ranch house.

The bones were obviously larger than those of modern bison or cattle but no one at the ranch was particularly interested in them. Many years passed and finally someone became mildly interested in the bones and gave them to Mr. Ed Price, of Raton, New Mexico. Again the years passed and it was not until 1925 that the bones once more attracted attention. In that year a number were sent to the Colorado Museum of Natural History and the paleontologists recognized them for what they were — the bones of an extinct bison. Thousands of years ago the bison had roamed the plains of North America. They were tremendous, long-horned animals, larger than our present-day bison.

In order to obtain some of the ancient skeletons the museum sent expeditions to Folsom, New Mexico, and during three summers the men dug the great bones out of the arroyo bank. When

Park visitors entering Balcony House on ranger-guided tour

147

the digging was finished, the men had recovered thirty skeletons of the long-extinct bison. But in addition, they had found something far more important. Among the bison bones they had discovered nineteen beautiful dart, or spear points. The points were so closely associated with the bones that there could be no doubt as to their antiquity. And, with equal certainty, there could be no doubt that ancient hunters had killed the great bison.

All evidence indicated that a few thousand years ago this was a swampy, boggy place, a bison wallow. Primitive hunters crept up on the drowsing animals and sometimes made a kill. They skinned the bison, cut off what meat they wanted and left the carcasses to rot in the mud. Sometimes they failed to extract all of their dart points from the bodies of the bison. As the centuries passed the bones became deeply covered with earth and there they remained until that fateful day when Nigger George rode by.

Geologists who studied the Folsom Site felt that the bison bones had been there in the earth at least twelve or fifteen thousand years. The importance of the nineteen dart points was immediately evident. Since they had caused the death of the bison there could be no doubt that men were in the area twelve or fifteen thousand years ago. Before the Folsom discovery archeologists had felt that men had been in America only a short time. Now they were forced to revise their thinking concerning the antiquity of the American Indian.

When the Folsom discovery was announced many archeologists began searching for evidences of Folsom Man and a burning question was always in their minds. Who would have the honor of finding Folsom Man himself? After twenty-five years of searching, the question is still unanswered. Folsom Man still evades his trackers for no skeletons have been found which can be considered, without doubt, to have belonged to him.

Evidences are plentiful for in many parts of the United States the points have been found. But Folsom Man himself still eludes us. The name means little. It is a term that is rather loosely applied to the makers of the beautiful Folsom Points. They are entirely distinctive and are among the highest examples of the flint workers art that have been found in America. Beautifully shaped, delicately chipped points with grooved faces, they can not be confused with any other dart or spear points. They have been found in many places, often associated with the bones of extinct animals.

Up in northern Colorado, near the town of Fort Collins, is the Lindenmeier Site. In it were found the bones of the same bison as those of Folsom. With them were the same Folsom Points. With them, also, were stone knives, scrapers, chopping and rubbing stones, as well as the ashes and charcoal from ancient campfires. They were spread over a large area. It was a camp-site where Folsom Man actually had lived. Was Folsom Man in camp? No, he had stepped out!

In Nebraska, Kansas, Oklahoma, Texas and other states, sim-ilar finds have been made. Folsom Points, and other points equally ancient, have been found in association with the bones of many extinct animals such as the bison, horse, mammoth and camel. Everywhere are found the evidences; nowhere is found Folsom Man himself.

Bones of the extinct animals, being solid and massive, have lasted well. Tools made of stone last indefinitely. Human bones, being thin and delicate, disintegrate more rapidly. There were probably few burials in those days and the human bones were scattered to the four winds. Still the search goes on. Sooner or later the find will be made. In the back of a dry cave some-where in the Southwest, probably, will be found some human bones. With them will be some Folsom Points. Then we will know that the points and the bones belonged to the same man — Folsom Man.

Or perhaps, when the human bones are found, a Folsom Point will actually be sticking in one of them. Then we will be sure that we have Folsom Man or, at least, someone whom Folsom Man did not like.

Although the actual physical remains of Folsom Man have not been found, a human skeleton, seemingly equally ancient, has recently been discovered. In 1947, scientists began exca-vating in a dry lake bed near Mexico City because of reports that natives had been finding mammoth bones in the area. Near the point where the mammoth bones had been found was discov-ered the partial skeleton of a man. The men who made the dis-covery were very sure the skeleton was as old as the layer of earth in which it was found, and this age was estimated to be 15,000 years.

Some scientists have been skeptical about the age of this skeleton, known as Tepexpan Man, feeling that it may represent a more recent burial. Recently, however, another discovery has been made which adds strength to the belief that Tepexpan Man is ancient. Early in 1952, the skeleton of a mammoth was found only a mile from the place where the human skeleton had been discovered. With the mammoth bones were found six man-made stone implements. One of these, a spear or dart point, was between two ribs of the mammoth - in all probability the animal had been killed by man. Even more important, however, was the fact that the human skeleton and the mammoth skeleton were found in the same layer of earth.

The importance of these two discoveries is obvious. The mammoth skeleton and the accompanying man-made implements indicate that man and mammoth lived in the area at the same time. The fact that the human and mammoth skeletons were found in the same layer of earth indicates that they may be equally ancient, and geologists feel that layer of earth was deposited about 15,000 years ago.

Thus, Tepexpan Man, unless grave errors were made during excavation, may well be the oldest human skeleton yet found in America. And the important point is that there was nothing primitive about this ancient man. He was a fully developed human being — Homo sapiens. In appearance he was much like men of today and his brain was almost as large as that of the average modern man.

The search for America's earliest inhabitants continues year after year. During the past twenty-five years many finds have been made but little has been learned about the people themselves. In each case, when an important find is made, it consists of spear points, dart points or other stone implements associated with the bones of extinct animals.

The Folsom Points, because of the importance of the original discovery, have received the greatest amount of publicity, but dart or spear points of many types have been found. Usually these projectile points are named because of the place where they are discovered and as a result there are Scottsbluff Points, Eden Points, Plainview Points, Sandia Points, and many more. The great need, at the present time, is for skeletal remains of the early men themselves. Some ancient human remains have been found but scientists are not in complete agreement as to their age. Even the Tepexpan skeleton, which may be the most important of all, has not been accepted by all of the men who are working on the problem of early man in America.

The story is being carried farther and farther into the past by stronger and stronger evidences. No one knows where it will end. Certain it is that America was discovered a great many thousands of years ago. Columbus was a late comer and he came the hard way. The real discoverers of America came the easy way: they just walked over.

All of the early inhabitants of America lived by hunting and fishing and by gathering the fruits, nuts, roots, berries and seeds which nature offered. Since they lived a roaming, drifting life, they built no permanent structures and as a result, their remains are not easily found. Because of this there are many question marks in the early part of the story and much is yet to be learned about the earliest inhabitants of the Americas.

As long as the early Indians lived a wandering, hunting life there was no real progress and we must come down to comparatively recent times in order to appreciate the greatest accomplishments of the American Indian. A short time ago, only a few thousand years at most, a very important thing happened. Somewhere in Mexico or Central America, perhaps in South America, the first farmers appeared. Some ancient Burbank produced corn, the plant which was responsible for all of the highest Indian cultures which the white man found when he blundered into America.

The origin of corn is still a mystery. For many years botanists have tried to trace it back to its wild plant ancestors but the entire story is still not known. Corn has moved so far and has changed so radically that there are gaps in the story and we may never know exactly how the Indians developed it. Certainly it was the most important food plant the Indians ever knew and because of it the lives of many Indians underwent a radical change.

Corn spread from one tribe to the next. One group after another found that farming was more dependable than hunting. Farther and farther it spread until large portions of North and South America were covered with farming Indians. With corn went other food plants which the Indians developed; beans, squash potatoes, tomatoes, and many more. Farming was in America to stay.

The result was amazing. Many Indians who formerly had followed the forest trails year after year now began to live settled lives. With dependable supplies of food coming from each harvest it was no longer necessary to move about. Permanent habitations soon appeared and villages and towns developed. The population increased and people began to concentrate in the best farming areas. With all this came new inventions which led the people always to higher stages of development.

When the white man finally arrived in 1492, there were fifteen or twenty million Indians in North and South America. Some still lived by hunting, some by fishing, others by gathering the seeds, roots and other plant products offered by nature. But millions of the Indians were highly developed agricultural people. The Pueblo Indians of the Southwest, the Indians of the New England states whom our first colonists met, the Mayas and Aztecs of Mexico, the Incas of South America, and many others had made surprising progress in a comparatively short time.

Credit for this progress goes to the amazing plant, corn, the American Indian's greatest single contribution to modern man.

10

ARCHEOLOGY OF THE MESA VERDE

A little while ago we spent a year with the people of Cliff Palace and we saw them at the peak of their development as far as the Mesa Verde was concerned. They were successful farmers, their arts and crafts were highly developed and their religious and social customs were rigid and complex. Obviously the people could not have achieved such a high cultural level in a short time: surely there must have been a long period of development in order for them to reach the stage we saw at Cliff Palace.

Actually this development extended over many centuries and we shall now take a little time to consider the events of that long period. This is the dry part of the story. When we saw the people in Cliff Palace they were warm, living beings, experiencing all the emotions any people may have. But now there will be no flesh on the bones and we shall deal only with the dead, rather dry facts archeologists dig out of the earth. So we shall not tarry too long.

About 2000 years ago farming Indians moved into the Mesa Verde region. The exact date is still unknown but it appears they were well established in some parts of the area by the beginning of the Christian Era. Even at that early date they were farmers and their progress is easy to follow. In the preceding chapter, covering the early history of the American Indian, we were dealing with elusive hunters. We saw not a single Indian; only dim, mysterious shapes sifting through a forest of question marks. But now we are dealing with farmers and we shall have solid substance on which to build our story.

The trail of farmers is easier to follow. They have a dependable food supply and live in one spot for generations. They build villages and cities, and best of all, excellent garbage piles. Nothing delights the archeologist as much as a big pile of trash for every piece is a paragraph in the story of a people. If he can find the things people have used, worn out and discarded the archeologist can reconstruct their lives to an amazing degree. Hunters seldom pile up their trash but farmers are more obliging. Living for generations in a village they carry it outside and dump it in one nice big pile. And in those successive layers of trash is the story of the people. The archeologist revels in it. Except for the professional garbage collector he is probably the only person in the world who is thankful for trash.

Excavation of ruins and trash piles has revealed that the Mesa Verde region was occupied by farming Indians from about the beginning of the Christian Era, possibly somewhat earlier, until almost 1300 A. D. For convenience this long occupation has been divided into four archeological periods. Actually there were no abrupt breaks between these periods. Once the farming Indians settled in the area they developed steadily and there was constant progress until the climax was reached.

Dividing the occupation into periods makes it much easier, however, to follow the progress of the people. Various archeologists have used different names for the periods but we shall use a system that was developed by Dr. Frank H. H. Roberts, of the Smithsonian Institution. Dates for the various periods vary somewhat in different parts of the Pueblo area but those used here serve well for the Mesa Verde itself.

Basket Maker Period. 1 to 450 A. D.
Modified Basket Maker Period. 450 to 750 A. D.
Developmental Pueblo Period. 750 to 1100 A. D.
Great Pueblo Period. 1100 to 1300 A. D.

The fact that the first two periods are called "Basket Maker" and the last two "Pueblo" should not be considered as an indication that there was a difference in the people themselves. Many years ago it was felt that during the eighth century there was a change in the physical type but this idea has been discarded. The people as well as their culture seem to have progressed in an unbroken line. It should be noted, also, that the dates are not rigid and they do not indicate abrupt, easily discerned cultural changes.

BASKET MAKER PERIOD. 1 to 450 A. D.

The Basket Makers were the earliest farmers in the Mesa Verde area. Their culture was comparatively simple and was featured by excellent weaving, especially of baskets and bags. Because of this trait they were called Basket Makers by the early explorers and the name has stuck. Credit for recognizing and naming these early people goes to Richard Wetherill, whom we have already met. In 1893, the Wetherills were digging in a great cave in Butler Wash, in southeastern Utah. While digging in the natural sand floor of the cave Richard found a burial pit, then another and another. When the excavation of the cave was completed the Wetherills had found ninety burials and in many cases the bodies were well mummified because of the drying effect of the cave sand.

The men were immediately impressed by the fact that the ninety graves had yielded no pottery. Previously they had excavated extensively in the Mesa Verde where the graves always contained pottery. But not a single piece was found with the burials in Butler Wash. Instead, the burials yielded a profusion of baskets. For this reason Richard began referring to the people as the "Basket Makers" and the name is still in use.

Few evidences of the early Basket Makers have been found in the Mesa Verde. The remains of these people are found in caves and Mesa Verde caves contain cliff dwellings. In order to find the early remains it will be necessary to excavate under the cliff dwellings and this work is yet to be done. However, the Basket Makers seem to have occupied the entire Mesa Verde region and when it becomes possible to excavate under the cliff dwellings the material probably will be found. Even though few evidences of the Basket Makers have been discovered in the Mesa Verde the culture is well known from extensive excavation in nearby areas.

At the beginning of the Basket Maker period the people seem to have lived a seminomadic life. They had only recently taken up farming and at first they probably farmed incidentally, regarding it only as a novel side line. Its possibilities became more and more apparent with each harvest and conditions were soon reversed. Farming became the mainstay and hunting became the side line. After the people fully realized the advantages of agriculture they never returned to a hunting life. Their main dependence was on the harvests and hunting was secondary in importance.

Our first recognition of these people brings up an interesting problem. Were they living in the Mesa Verde region as hunters when corn and squash came to them from some other tribe or did they bring these plants from some other region where they had already learned to farm? The answer is not yet known so we can simply say that when we first recognize them in the Mesa Verde area they were turning from a hunting to a farming life.

Physically, the Basket Makers were an interesting group. A large number of their burials have been found so their physical appearance is not in doubt. They were rather short in stature, the women averaging about five feet and the men three or four inches taller. The skin color varied from light to dark brown and it is safe to say that their eyes were also brown. The hair was black, sometimes rusty black and occasionally was inclined toward a slight waviness. On the mummies that have been found the hair of the women usually is cropped short but the male mummies sometimes exhibit elaborate hair styling. On some a wide line was shaved down the center of the head and the remaining hair was done up in a number of large and small braids.

If we could have walked through a Basket Maker village we probably would have considered the people rather attractive even when viewed from our own standards. They would have seemed short to us but well proportioned. Their features would have been pleasing for there would have been none of the amazing skull deformities which we saw among the people of Cliff Palace. Everything indicates they were a peaceful, easygoing people and, in all probability, they would have been easy to like.

From a cultural viewpoint the Basket Makers are important because of their lack of certain very important traits. During their early farming stages they did not make pottery, did not use the bow and arrow, and did not have permanent houses except in one area which we shall mention in a moment.

The lack of houses and pottery was perfectly natural for they had only recently been a hunting people. While they lived as hunters they were forced to move about in search of game and a permanent house was an impossibility. Pottery was also out of the question for it was too heavy for them to transport as they moved about. The absence of the bow was simply due to the fact that it had not yet reached these people. The bow probably was invented only once. From its point of beginning somewhere in the Old World it spread slowly from tribe to tribe and we shall see it reach the Basket Makers at a later date.

All people need shelter, household utensils and weapons so, lacking houses, pottery and the bow, our Basket Makers used substitutes. As is always the case they were inferior.

Part of the time, probably during the cold seasons, the Basket Makers lived in caves. These offered shelter from the elements and provided safe, dry places for the storage of food. The women built their fires in level sheltered areas and around these fires centered most of the activities. In the rear of the cave they constructed storage cists for their corn. Small pits were dug in the cave floor and were lined with slabs of sandstone chinked with bark and mud. Over the pit was placed a roof of poles and packed earth, leaving only a small hatchway which was closed with a thin stone slab. Such cists were secure and dry and served as excellent storage bins for the year's harvest of corn. When the people left the cave for any length of time they could conceal the storage pits by covering them over with earth and stones so they would not be detected by chance visitors.

Even though most of the Basket Maker remains have been found in caves it is probable that they lived in the open near their fields for at least part of the year. As farming became more important to them they were forced to protect their crops. Each farm needed to be watched carefully to prevent damage by birds and mammals or even by men of other groups. Because of this necessity of living near their fields it is probable that they erected temporary shelters for protection from the sun and rain. A mere framework of poles covered with brush and grass would have sufficed. No trace of these temporary shelters has been found but there is a strong feeling that they did exist.

Recent excavations have revealed that in one area the Basket Makers began experimenting with permanent houses at an earlier date than formerly had been realized. Near Durango, Colorado, Mr. Earl H. Morris, of the Carnegie Institution, excavated a number of house structures, both in caves and on open hillsides, which date from the first and second centuries A. D. While these houses were crude when compared with the standardized pithouses which later came into wide use, they do indicate that the Basket Makers, in that area at least, began to experiment with permanent structures soon after they became a farming people. Further excavation may reveal that crude, hogan-like structures were in general use at an earlier date than has been realized.

The absence of pottery during Basket Maker times resulted in a widespread use of baskets and, as the name implies, basketry was the major craft. Many of the baskets of this period are superb examples of workmanship and design. Skillfully woven, artistically decorated and gracefully shaped they are outstanding among the basketry of the early Indians. Shallow trays were the most common form but there were also bowls, water baskets, deep carrying baskets and small baskets which probably served for storing trinkets and ceremonial objects. Large, flexible bags were also woven and these were often split open and used as burial wrappings.

Since pottery was unknown baskets were used for all household purposes where containers were needed. Some were so tightly woven that water could be carried and stored in them and, surprisingly, food was cooked in them. Cooking in a basket was a tedious affair. Stones were placed in the fire and when they were very hot were dropped into the basket of food. When the stones cooled they were replaced with more hot stones until the cook's fingers were thoroughly burned and her patience was exhausted. Half-cooked "stew-a-la-ashes" was the inevitable result. It was a crude, inefficient method and greatly limited the cooking possibilities.

Lack of the bow and arrow forced the Basket Makers to rely on an odd weapon, the atlatl, which was as difficult to use as it is to pronounce. It was used in many parts of the world before the bow took its place. The atlatl was a spear thrower which served as a mechanical lengthener for the arm. It was a slender, flattened stick about two feet in length. At one end was the grip, equipped with two loops for the fingers. At the opposite end, on the upper face, was a short spur or hook, against which the dart or spear rested.

The dart, either a reed or a slender shaft of wood, was four or five feet long. One end was tipped with a stone point: the other end was feathered and this basal end was cup-shaped to fit against the spur on the atlatl. In reality the dart was merely a long arrow.

When the hunter was ready to use the atlatl he held it in his hand with his first two fingers through the finger loops. The end of the dart was hooked against the spur at the rear end of the atlatl and the arm was drawn back with the atlatl extending out behind, horizontally. From this position the arm was thrown sharply forward in a long sweeping arc and the dart was projected from the end of the atlatl. In this way the length of the arm was doubled and great force was imparted to the missle.

Even though the atlatl was a powerful weapon it had certain bad points. Accuracy was difficult to achieve and it was not well adapted for use in stalking game. The hunter was forced to stand erect and be free of bushes and trees in order to throw the dart. Later we shall see the people discard the atlatl in favor of a superior weapon.

In addition to the atlatl another wooden implement was in common use. This was a short, curved stick about two feet long which was much like the throwing stick used by modern Hopis in killing rabbits. While the exact use of the curved stick is not known the fact that it is so often found with the atlatl must indicate that the two comprised the hunting or fighting equipment of the men.

The atlatl was a poor weapon for use in hunting small game so nets and snares were widely used. The nets, made of yucca fiber and human hair cord, were sometimes over two hundred feet long and three or four feet wide. Such nets probably were stretched across game trails or small canyons and the game was driven into them by groups of men who would then club the trapped animals. Dogs, which the people seem to have had from the very first, may have been used in the game drives. These were not just tamed wolves or coyotes, but true dogs which had been brought across from Asia.

Clothing of the Basket Makers can best be described as scanty. A great many well-preserved mummies have been found and since it was customary to place the personal possessions of the deceased in the grave we can assume that no articles of clothing have escaped us completely. The total wardrobe seems to have consisted of robes and sandals for people of all ages and, occasionally, small string aprons for the women.

The Basket Maker country was cold in winter, temperatures sometimes dropping as low as zero. Since there were few, if any, houses except in the one area mentioned above, some articles of clothing were needed during the winter months. In every case these seem to have been robes made of animal skins. Sometimes they were simply the tanned hides of deer, mountain sheep or elk. The finest robes, however, were woven from strips of fur. Rabbit skins were cut into long narrow strips which were wound around yucca cords to produce fur-covered strings. These were woven into robes which, when wrapped around the body, gave the wearer considerable protection against the winter's cold. Beautiful sashes were woven from dog hair and these probably were used to hold the robes and blankets in place.

Sandals evidently were common for a great many have been found in Basket Maker caves. These were woven of yucca fibers or yucca fiber cords and consisted simply of a square-toed, flat sole which was held to the foot by tie strings.

The only other article of clothing was a small string apron worn by the women. This consisted of a cord or belt which was tied around the waist and from this hung scores or hundreds of strings. The fringe of strings was only a few inches wide so it evidently covered only the front of the wearer. Sometimes the strings were long enough to pass between the legs and be looped over the waist band at the back. The number of aprons found is not large and it may indicate that they were worn only at times of occasional necessity.

Present evidence indicates that except for sandals the Basket Makers wore little clothing during the warm season. When winter came the fur and skin robes, of which there seem to have been an abundance, provided protection from the cold.

What the people lacked in clothing they made up in jewelry. Beads, necklaces, pendants and earrings are found in profusion in the graves and there can be no doubt that the people had a strong desire for personal adornment. The materials used seem quite drab to us but from such ordinary materials as shell, bone, seeds and brightly-colored stones, jewelry of lasting beauty was fashioned.

An ancient style show

Left. These superb, 1500-year old sashes are made of dog hair
Right. Necklaces made of bone, stone and shells

The Basket Maker cradle was entirely different from the wooden cradle we saw used in Cliff Palace. It was a soft flexible affair made of reeds and withes. A long stick was bent into a loop and the ends were tied together to form an oval frame. To this was bound a layer of reeds or slender withes and the cradle was then padded with soft bark or fur. When the baby was bound to the cradle a soft pad was placed under its head and the skull developed normally without being flattened.

Many additional tools of wood, stone and bone are found when Basket Maker caves are excavated: wooden planting sticks and scoops; stone knives, scrapers, drills and pipes; bone awls, scrapers and whistles. An important item was the metate, or milling stone. This was a slab of stone with a shallow trough on the top surface. Corn was placed on the metate and ground with the mano, a small stone which was rubbed back and forth in the trough.

One of the interesting things about the Basket Makers was the manner in which they buried their dead and, surprisingly enough, it is because of this that we have our present knowledge of the early people. All burials which have been found up to the present time have been found in caves, although it is possible that bodies were sometimes buried in other places. A favorite place for burial seems to have been the cists which originally were built for the storage of food. When these were not available graves were dug in the cave floor or the bodies were placed in holes and crevices in the rocks. Often several bodies were buried together and as many as nineteen have been found in a single grave. The bodies were flexed, with the arms and legs drawn up against the chest. Blankets were wrapped around them and sometimes the burial bundle was placed in a large woven bag.

Fortunately for the archeologist it was customary to place offerings in the grave and these consisted of articles the deceased had used or articles his spirit would need in the afterworld. Even though burial took place almost 2000 years ago the dry caves have preserved the materials amazingly well and as a result we have not only the mummified remains of the people but all of the articles which were in daily use centuries ago.

We have seen briefly the outstanding traits of the Basket Maker culture. Summing them up, we see a tribe of Indians living in the Mesa Verde region at the beginning of the Christian

Era. Formerly hunters, they turned more and more to farming, raising corn and squash on the mesa tops or in open canyon bottoms. Having no permanent houses they sought the shelter of caves and since pottery was unknown baskets were widely used. The atlatl, or spear thrower, was used instead of the bow. Minor arts and crafts enabled the people to live a comparatively well-rounded life.

The noteworthy point is that from this simple beginning developed the amazing Pueblo culture which reached its peak in the thirteenth century. Since the people were industrious and intelligent they progressed steadily, following the same trail which all people have taken in their climb toward civilization. In the early stages progress was slow but with the acquisition of each new idea the pace quickened.

The great step forward was the abandonment of the chase, the acceptance of a settled farming life. Within a short time they became firmly established agriculturists. Their main dependence for food was soon on their farms, and wild animals and plants became a secondary source.

The change to a farming life revolutionized the entire culture. As the source of food changed the religious, social and economic life also changed. The religion of hunters could never suffice for farmers. The men viewed rain, snow, the soil, the sun, frosts and the changing seasons through the eyes of farmers instead of through the eyes of hunters. All events of nature were interpreted according to their effect upon agriculture. New social regulations grew out of the settled existence and the entire outlook on life was different.

Even though progress was slow at first some startling changes came. About the middle of the fifth century some of the changes were so important that the culture was radically modified. A new descriptive term must now be used in order to indicate these new developments.

MODIFIED BASKET MAKER PERIOD. 450 to 750 A. D.

Even though the culture changed the people themselves did not. It is extremely important to keep in mind the fact that the Modified Basket Makers were merely the descendants of the true Basket Makers. They added new material things to their culture, thus modifying it, but they themselves changed not one particle.

To state it briefly, it can be said that the change in name has been made because the people acquired the things which were mentioned as lacking during the earlier period. They learned to make pottery, they began to build houses and they adopted the bow and arrow. Thus the true basket making culture changed. The weaving of baskets continued but the addition of pottery modified the culture and this is indicated in the new name.

It is important to note that all three of the new developments did not appear at exactly the same time nor did they reach all of the Basket Makers at the same time. They spread from one group to the next. They were slow in getting to some regions or, since there are conservatives among all people, perhaps some of the Basket Makers were hesitant about accepting the new-fangled contraptions.

It is extremely doubtful if the Basket Makers invented a single one of the important new things. New inventions usually were passed from one tribe to another: often an intricate contrivance such as the bow and arrow traveled all over the world after a single invention. The Basket Makers did a certain amount of traveling and trading and they were not averse to borrowing new ideas from their neighbors.

It seems fairly certain that pottery came to them from the south where other tribes had been making it prior to its arrival in the Mesa Verde region. Some of the Basket Maker men, while on a trading expedition, may have seen women making vessels out of clay. Realizing the superiority of these vessels which could be placed directly on the fire the men mentioned the matter to their wives upon their return home. Possessed only of the idea, the women began trying to make pottery.

They were practically forced to invent pottery all over again for they knew nothing about the actual process. They had merely heard that fine vessels could be made from clay. Their first attempts were extremely clumsy and resulted in absolute failure. They made the first pots from pure clay and as fast as it dried the vessels cracked and fell into pieces. After a time the women realized they must add something to the clay to hold it together. Straw and juniper bark were tried and there was a certain measure of success. The vessels had less tendency to crack but when they were placed on the fire the straw burned out and the result was more in the nature of a sieve than a pot.

The patient women continued to experiment and at last they learned that some kind of sand or grit was necessary for temper. In several places in the Mesa Verde volcanic formations provided the potters with an abundance of volcanic grit. When this was ground fine and added to the pottery clay the vessels did not crack upon drying. The first pieces of pottery were merely sun dried but soon the women learned that if they were subjected to intense heat they were much stronger and were waterproof. Each vessel was carefully baked, or fired, and true pottery was the result.

The effect of pottery upon the food habits of the people was profound. With vessels that could be placed directly on the fire whole new lines of food were available. Soups, stews, porridges and greens became commonplace. Many new plants were utilized and innumerable combinations of meats and plants were discovered. Pottery was also of great value for water storage. Baskets were not good for this because the moisture soon caused them to disintegrate. Pottery lasted indefinitely and each woman could make an unlimited number of large water jars. On rainy days every jar in the village could be filled and the terrors of drouth were lessened.

Thus it is easily seen that the perfection of pottery was one of the major steps in the progress of the Indians. The diet was improved, the drudgery of cooking was lessened, the range of foods was widened, storage facilities were increased and the entire domestic economy of the people took a decided turn for the better.

At first the pottery was crude but with each succeeding generation it improved. The proper percentage of temper and clay was discovered, designs were introduced and improved upon and vessel shapes became more graceful and efficient. As time passed the fingers of the potters became more and more deft.

The adoption of a permanent house was also of great importance. Life in the open caves was never too comfortable. Heavy rains, deep snows and the bitter temperatures of winter held certain terrors for the people who were without actual dwellings. No great population could ever grow under such conditions. A permanent, secure house was needed to stabilize the culture.

As we have already seen, the Basket Makers in at least one area began to experiment with permanent houses at an early date. It is not yet known whether these earliest houses developed into the standardized pithouses which spread widely over the area early in Modified Basket Maker times but we may be quite sure the people did not develop it entirely by themselves. Similar pithouses were used by Indians in many parts of America, in fact they can be traced up the northwest coast and on to Alaska and Siberia. Since this type of house was used so widely it is probable that the Basket Makers borrowed the idea from some neighboring tribe.

The dwellings were pithouses, partially above and partially below the ground. The underground portion consisted of a shallow pit two or three feet in depth and ten to twenty feet in diameter. Sometimes the earthen walls were plastered with clay, or if the walls had a tendency to cave they were lined with stone slabs. In the floor, forming a large square, four holes were dug and a forked post slightly higher than a man's head was set upright in each. Four slender logs were placed in the forks of these posts forming a square framework, the main support of the roof. Slender poles were slanted from the edge of the pit to this framework at twelve or fifteen inch intervals, entirely around the room. Other poles were placed across the flat, top portion to complete the skeleton of the roof.

To this framework was lashed a solid covering of reeds, brush, bark or coarse grass and the entire roof was covered with a layer of earth several inches thick. A small hatchway was left in the center of the roof. This served as a smoke hole and it was often equipped with a ladder and used as an entrance. The firepit was in the center of the room below the smoke hole.

Since the pithouse needed ventilation a tunnel was dug through the south wall and brought to the surface a few feet south of the house. Sometimes this tunnel served merely as a ventilator and crawl entrance but usually the end was enlarged into a room. This second room was always smaller than the main room but it was roofed in much the same manner. In reality a house of this type consisted of the large main room and a smaller antechamber, the two being connected by a tunnel. The location of the antechamber door is uncertain. Probably there was a hatchway in the roof or there may have been a door in one of the side walls. It is certain that the fire in the main room drew fresh air from the antechamber for just in front of the tunnel entrance was placed a large stone slab which served as a deflector. This slab kept the current of fresh air from blowing across the fire and, in the winter, prevented cold air from sweeping across the floor where people were sleeping.

The sipapu, a small hole in the floor near the firepit, made its appearance at this time. This feature has continued in use to the present day for some of the modern Pueblo Indians have similar holes in the floors of their kivas. It serves as a symbolic entrance to the Mother Earth and its importance is indicated by the fact that it has persisted for so many centuries.

Many of the earliest pithouses, perhaps the very first ones, were built in caves. The people had used the caves for centuries and it was only natural that they should build houses there. Within a short time, however, there was a movement toward the open country and soon pithouse villages were being built on the mesa tops and in open valleys. The caves, although they provided shelter from the winter's storms, were cold and uncomfortable for the sun shone in only a few hours each day. With substantial houses the people no longer feared the rigors of winter and life in the open was far more pleasant than in the cold, shadowy caves. By the seventh century most of the people seem to have moved out of the caves and they were seldom used until the time when the cliff dwellings were built.

One of the far-reaching effects of the permanent house was its influence on true family life. Before this time the people probably had lived in haphazard groups with little opportunity for development of the true family. The house changed all this. In most instances a small pithouse probably served as the dwelling place of a single family and this gave new meaning to the family as a compact unit. Family ties, relationships and inheritance probably took on new meanings.

As generations passed the houses improved and toward the end of the period an important development came. For some time the people had built slab-lined storage rooms around their pithouses. At first they were small but gradually they were enlarged until they could serve as living rooms. The floor was slightly below ground level and the walls of the pit were lined with stone slabs. The above-ground walls were built of poles and adobe and the flat roof was of similar materials. The rooms became rectangular and the side walls vertical making it possible to join them together in long rows. At the end of the period many of the villages consisted of long rows of living rooms in front of which were a few of the old-type pithouses. These pithouses grew deeper and gradually seem to have developed into ceremonial rooms. This was the beginning of the kiva, a subterranean room which is still used for this purpose by present-day Pueblo Indians. Ruins of the type described above are called slab-house villages because of the stone slabs which lined the walls of the living rooms.

The third cultural trait which set the Modified Basket Makers apart from their ancestors, the Basket Makers, was the bow and arrow. Again the people borrowed. The bow and arrow is such a complicated combination that it is easier to believe it was invented once, then spread over the world, than that it was invented several times by different people. The invention occurred in the Old World and the weapon was brought to America by many bands of immigrants.

The Indians of the Mesa Verde received the bow and arrow after they had acquired houses and pottery. Some band of wandering Indians probably brought the new weapon into the region and the people may have obtained it by peaceful borrowing. Or they may have recognized the superiority of the bow through the sad experience of trying to defend themselves with their atlatls. Whatever the circumstances may have been they adopted the bow and the atlatl was discarded.

The bow excelled the atlatl in every way. It had greater accuracy and was well adapted for stalking game or defending the home since it could be shot from almost any position. Brush and trees did not interfere with its use as in the case of the atlatl which could be used only where there was room for the overhead sweep of the arm. Arrows were shorter than atlatl darts, easier to carry and their range was greater. The bow was also more efficient in the killing of small game.

As is always the case the old gave way to the new. The bow was accepted and soon mastered. Defense of the home was easier, hunting was more efficient and more game animals were killed than had been possible with the atlatl.

An extremely important point that must be remembered is that the house, pottery and the bow did not all arrive at the same time. It must not be considered that on a certain day, in a certain year, the Basket Makers voted to accept the new things and become Modified Basket Makers. These new cultural traits filtered in slowly and the people themselves little realized how their culture was changing.

During this period beans came up from the south and were accepted eagerly by the farmers. It is entirely possible that this acceptance was made possible by the new cooking vessels which the people now possessed. At an altitude of 7000 feet dry beans require several hours of boiling and while the people cooked in baskets this would have been virtually impossible. Pottery cooking vessels made the task easy, however, and the beans, an excellent protein food, gave the people a more balanced diet. New varieties of corn also appeared. Previously only red corn had been grown but now other colors became common.

During this period other cultural changes of a minor nature occurred. Hafted stone mauls and axes appeared, the latter being vitally necessary for cutting the many poles used in house construction. The turkey was domesticated and feather blankets, which had first appeared in the preceding period, became increasingly common. Jewelry was much the same as in earlier times except that turquoise came into use and this gave the people an additional stone from which to make beads, pendants and earrings.

The popularity of baskets was in no way lessened by the appearance of pottery and some of the finest baskets were made at this time. Sandals improved in quality and the shape changed slightly. In the preceding period the sandals were square-toed but now the toe became V-shaped, or scalloped. Often the sandals were elaborately decorated with colored designs and with designs produced by variations in the weave.

There is much evidence that the culture became more and more stabilized with each succeeding generation. Farming methods improved and the harvests became more abundant. With dependable supplies of food, the added comfort and security of the dwellings and the improvement of living conditions the population increased. By the early part of the eighth century a large population of farming Indians occupied the Mesa Verde and surrounding regions. It must have been a peaceful time for the villages were widely scattered over the mesas and open valleys, evidently with little thought of concentration for safety.

Ruins of this period are found in abundance in the Mesa Verde. Scores of pithouse and slab-house villages have been found on the mesa tops and one pithouse village has been found in a cave. In most cases pithouses which were built in caves are now underneath the cliff dwellings which were built later. Step House Cave, however, proved to be an exception. In this cave, located in Long Canyon, the cliff dwelling occupies only the north end of the cave leaving a large clear space at the south end. This area was covered with several feet of trash which the occupants of the cliff dwelling had thrown out. In 1926, Supt. Jesse L. Nusbaum excavated under this trash layer and found three pithouses which had been built about 600 A. D. This discovery indicates that some of the early pithouses were built in caves and that excavation under some of the cliff dwellings should reveal further evidence of cave occupation during Modified Basket Maker times.

DEVELOPMENTAL PUEBLO PERIOD.   750 to 1100 A. D.

As we move into this new period it should be stressed that there was no radical change in the culture. The same people continued to occupy the Mesa Verde and they showed the same progressive tendencies which we have seen in the earlier periods.

At this time, however, the people did a surprising thing. They adopted a new cradle. Offhand, this may not seem especially important but it had a startling effect and early archeologists were confronted with a baffling problem. The new cradle caused such a radical change in the appearance of the Indians that until recently the archeologists thought a new people had moved into the region.

When the Basket Makers first were recognized half a century ago it was noticed immediately that their skulls were strikingly different from those of the people who had lived in pueblos and cliff dwellings. Skulls of the Basket Makers were longer and narrower and there was no deformity on the back. In contrast, skulls of the later people were broad and this broadness was emphasized by a flattening on the back, a deformity caused by the hard cradle board. The head shape was so radically different that early archeologists assumed a new, broad-headed people had moved into the region during the eighth century and merged with the Basket Makers.

As southwestern archeology progressed through uncertain early years this assumption that the Basket Makers and Pueblos were two different people was generally accepted. In those early days there was not enough skeletal material for an exhaustive comparative study and while many questions were unanswered and doubts were often expressed by archeologists, the separate identity of the Basket Makers and Pueblos was generally accepted.

Now the story has changed. Recent intensive study of a large amount of skeletal material, ranging from the ancient Basket Makers to recent Pueblo Indians, has thrown new light on the problem. The result is that after all these years it now becomes apparent that there was no radical change of physical type at all. The Basket Maker type seems to have persisted with little evidence of any great addition of new blood.

The radical change in the shape of the heads seems to have resulted from the new cradle which the people adopted during the eighth century. The soft, padded cradle of the Basket Makers was discarded and within a short time all of the women of the tribe were using a cradle made of wood. No pillow was placed under the baby's head and the result was inevitable. The back of the head flattened, the sides bulged and a broad, deformed head resulted.

How can this change of cradles be explained except by saying that it was a craze, a new beauty fad which caught the fancy of the people. Where it came from is not known: surely it must have been borrowed from other people with whom the Basket Makers came in contact. Evidently the new head shape became fashionable for within a short time the new cradle was adopted throughout the area. Instead of changing the hat or "hairdo", as is the custom among modern people, they went to the very root of the matter and changed the shape of the skull itself.

From this time on we are going to know the people as Pueblo Indians. "Pueblo" is a Spanish word meaning village, or town, and was applied by the early Spaniards to Indians whom they

Pueblo cradle board

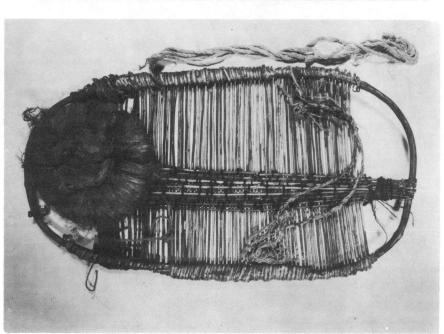

Basket Maker cradle

175

found living in large, compact, many-roomed villages. It is an excellent term, as far as architecture is concerned, for from the eighth century on the Indians of the Mesa Verde showed an increasing tendency to join their houses together to form compact villages. The term, Developmental Pueblo period, means exactly what it says. It was a time of development and expansion and during this period the groundwork was laid for the Great Pueblo period which followed.

Once again we should stress a very important point. Even though we have changed names, even though we have stepped from the Modified Basket Maker to the Developmental Pueblo period there was no abrupt cultural change. The only real difference as we move from one period to the next is in the appearance of the people. Because of the adoption of the hard cradle their heads became broad and deformed but otherwise the changes were gradual and it is difficult to draw a sharp line between the two periods.

During the Developmental Pueblo period there was the same gradual development in all lines that we have seen throughout the earlier periods. The people were alert and curious: they were energetic and ambitious and the result was steady development. It was a period of peace and the people seem to have lived without fear of an enemy. The caves were deserted and villages were built on the open mesa tops or in broad valleys near the fields of corn, beans and squash which provided them with food in abundance. The population grew rapidly and spread over a vast area in the Four Corners region where Colorado, Utah, Arizona and New Mexico now meet at a common point. It was a far-flung culture and there is every evidence that for a long time there was peace and prosperity among the people.

The most important development during this period was in the field of architecture. At the end of the previous period most of the villages consisted of groups of individual pithouses. Some of the villages, however, were made up of long curving rows of flat-roofed houses built of poles, stone slabs and adobe. In front of the living rooms were one or more pithouses which probably served as ceremonial rooms.

At first the Developmental Pueblo villages were merely continuations of these earlier villages. As time passed improvements came, indicating that the builders were doing a great deal of experimenting. Walls of many types were built and with each generation there was progress. During this period the population of the Mesa Verde evidently was large for the mesa tops are dotted with scores, perhaps hundreds, of ruins.

Recently five ruins dating from this period have been excavated in the Mesa Verde. Two of the ruins are at the Twin Trees site, with one ruin sitting on top of the other. The other three are less than three hundred yards away at Site 16. And here again the ruins are piled up one on top of another. The people showed a strong tendency to build villages on the ruins of earlier villages.

The five ruins, taken in chronological order, show very clearly the architectural progress of the Developmental Pueblo period:

850 A. D. The first ruin is a slab-house pueblo. The floors of the living rooms were a foot or more below ground level and the earthen walls were lined with slabs. The upper walls consisted of slender posts, set a few inches apart, with the intervening spaces filled with adobe. In front of the long row of living rooms were four pitrooms, each one being about six feet deep. The roof of each pitroom was supported on four posts set in the floor of the room.

900 A. D. The second ruin is a post-and-adobe pueblo. The floors of the living rooms were not dug below ground level and no stone slabs were used. The walls consisted of posts, set upright a foot or more apart. The spaces between the posts were filled with adobe into which had been forced many small stones. In front of the living rooms was a kiva of a very early type. The walls were of plastered native earth. The roof was supported on four posts but instead of rising from the kiva floor the posts were built into the face of a bench which encircled the room.

950 A. D. The third ruin is a small masonry pueblo. The walls were built of stones and adobe but the masonry was exceedingly crude. The stones were irregular in shape and only a few were laid in even rows. An excessive amount of adobe was used; actually the walls were about fifty percent adobe and fifty percent stone. In front of the living rooms was an early type kiva. The walls were of plastered native earth and

the roof, instead of being supported on posts, was supported on four stone pillars, or pilasters, which rested on the bench.

1000 A. D. The fourth ruin is a small pueblo built of single-coursed masonry. The walls of the living rooms contain stones which were well shaped but without smoothed faces. The stones were laid in even rows but the walls were only the thickness of a single stone, measuring less than a foot in width. The kiva, which was located in front of the living rooms, approached the standard Mesa Verde type. The walls below the bench were faced with stone and the roof was supported by six stone pilasters which rested on the bench.

1075 A. D. The fifth ruin is a pueblo built of thick, double-coursed masonry. The faces of the stones were smoothed and some retain the peck marks of the tools used in the shaping process. Some of the walls were two stories high. The kiva, located in front of the living rooms, was of excellent construction. The roof was supported on eight stone pillars which rested on the bench, and the walls, from the floor to the top of the pillars, were faced with masonry of good quality. One new architectural feature, the tower, appears in this ruin. There are three of these tall, circular structures – we shall consider them in a moment.

The five ruins demonstrate graphically the steady architectural progress of the Developmental Pueblo period. In the beginning the houses were crudely built of posts and adobe and the underground rooms, which may not have been entirely ceremonial at first, were merely deep pitrooms. At the end of the period the houses were of good masonry and the standard Mesa Verde kiva had developed. Certainly this development shows that the people were constantly experimenting and as a result the architecture improved steadily. During the latter part of the period few large pueblos were built. Usually a village consisted of a few living rooms joined together in a compact unit. A short distance south of the living rooms was a single kiva.

Pottery also made rapid advances during this period. The women had become convinced of its value and they experimented endlessly, probably in a spirit of friendly competition. During the preceding period pottery was dull gray in color and the crudely painted designs did not contrast well with this drab background. The women now learned to apply a thin wash of white clay to the vessels. This wash or slip, as it is called, produced a clear white background and against this the constantly improving designs stood out in bold contrast. Corrugated pottery appeared and vessels of this type were used chiefly for cooking purposes.

Good baskets still were made but pottery vessels were superior to baskets for most purposes. As a result the quality of the baskets began to decline. Sandals were much like those of earlier periods except that the toes were rounded and there was less elaborate decoration. Cotton came into use about the middle of the period and loom-woven cloth made its appearance. Recent experiments have indicated that cotton will not grow in the Mesa Verde so it must have been imported from warmer areas to the south.

Minor arts and crafts improved as the people became more proficient in the use of bone, stone and wood. An interesting change occurred in the metate, or milling stone, during this period. Earlier metates were trough-shaped, with a shallow groove for a grinding surface. Now a flat metate came into use and the entire surface was used for grinding the corn.

As the Developmental Pueblo period ended, thousands of peaceful farming Indians occupied the Mesa Verde and a vast area around it. The population had grown steadily since earliest Basket Maker times and the region may have known its greatest population at this time or in the early part of the following period. Most of the villages were small; usually they consisted of a few living rooms and a single kiva. These villages are often called unit pueblos and it has been suggested that each one may have housed a number of closely related families forming a single clan.

That the people were vigorous and ambitious is indicated by the progress which they made. Now we see them nearing their cultural peak and it is time for us to leave the Developmental Pueblo period and move into the golden age of the Pueblos.

GREAT, OR CLASSIC PUEBLO PERIOD. 1100 to 1300 A.D.

This period has often been called the golden age of the Pueblo people. Before we go into it, however, we should make some mention of the beginning date, 1100 A. D. Usually, in the general Pueblo area, an earlier date is given for the beginning of the period. One may very easily push it back fifty or one hundred years, or even more, depending upon how the period is defined.

Recent studies have produced some perplexing problems concerning the architecture, pottery and movements of the people during their last two or three centuries in the Mesa Verde. It is hoped that within a short time some or all of these problems will be solved. Since the uncertainties do exist we shall, for our purposes here, lean rather heavily on the term "classic," which is often applied to this climax period. The culture reached its classic development during the 1100 - 1300 A. D. period so we shall use those dates.

We saw the beginning of Pueblo development over a thousand years earlier when the first grain of corn was planted somewhere in the Mesa Verde region. From that simple beginning we have seen the culture develop steadily without a backward step. Now it has reached its peak and for two centuries we shall see the people enjoy the results of their long struggle for improvement. It is true that adverse influences will affect the people and will cause a radical change in their way of life. But this adversity will not affect the arts and crafts and superior workmanship will continue to the very end of the Mesa Verde occupation.

The massive stone walls were the finest ever built in the Mesa Verde. The stones were carefully cut and were laid in neat even courses. Many of the walls were smoothly plastered and often they were decorated with brightly colored designs. The villages were often very large: sometimes they contained scores of rooms and rose to a height of four stories. Ceremonial rooms were numerous: sometimes there were more than a score in a single village. They were built after a definite pattern, giving evidence of rigid ceremonial practices.

Pottery of the Great Pueblo period was superb with the women of each area specializing in certain shapes and designs. In the Mesa Verde the women produced pottery of two types, the corrugated vessels which were used for cooking and for storage of food and water, and the black-on-white bowls, jars, ladles, kiva jars and mugs which were used for other purposes. The decorated pottery was highly polished and the intricate and carefully balanced black designs stood out in sharp contrast against the glossy white background. For some unknown reason the potters used a different material for their pottery paint during this period. Previously they had used mineral paints in producing their designs but now they used paint made from plants. Thus the designs were simply carbon which the firing process burned into the surface of the vessels.

During the two Pueblo periods basketry declined both in popularity and in excellence. This is to be expected, however, for pottery had taken its place to a great extent and it was not as important as in Basket Maker times. Good baskets were still woven in Great Pueblo times but they were fewer and the lack of elaborate decorations probably indicates that their popularity was waning. Sandals were still widely used but they too declined in quality. Possibly the loss of quality in basketry affected this closely allied craft.

Cotton cloth, often decorated in several colors, was produced in abundance and exquisite jewelry was made from turquoise, shell, bone and other materials. Even the minor tools give evidence of patient industry and nimble fingers.

The Great Pueblo period was a remarkable climax to the many centuries of cultural development which we have just witnessed. As we study it, however, one significant fact is obvious. It was a period of regimentation with the people moving in certain well established grooves. Artists and craftsmen were highly skilled but they all followed the same patterns. There was little tendency on the part of the individual to strike out by himself and develop new things. Individual initiative was not strong and the religious and social life probably was rigidly regulated.

As archeologists endeavor to reconstruct the events of the Great Pueblo period they are confronted with some puzzling problems concerning the general way of life of the people. During the period the architectural layout of the villages changed, the villages increased in size and their location changed. In addition, the population began to decline and great areas which had long been occupied were deserted. At first glance it would seem that adverse conditions were affecting the people but more work must be done before all of the problems can be solved.

At the beginning of the period the population was widely scattered and most of the villages were small unit pueblos which have already been mentioned. The fact that the people lived in small scattered villages would in itself indicate that no danger threatened. Even more indicative of peaceful times is the fact that the kiva was located outside the village walls. The kiva, an underground room, was used primarily by the men. The only exit was a small hatchway in the roof and through this only one man could emerge at a time. If a raiding party had surprised a small village while the men were in the kiva during a ceremony or at night the results would have been tragic.

Early in the Great Pueblo period the people began to change the location of the kiva. Soon, in most cases at least, the kiva was placed inside the village and was surrounded by the houses. No longer was the underground room a death trap in case of a surprise raid.

At about the same time tall round towers came into use. Sometimes they were built at the outer walls of the pueblo but very often the tower was built beside the kiva and was connected with it by an underground tunnel. The round tower, which stood higher than the rest of the village, would have served admirably as a lookout tower and connecting it with the men's room would seem a natural development. It has been suggested that the tower may have had some ceremonial use since it was connected with the kiva. More practical, however, is the idea that it was a watch tower which resulted from a defensive need. Or, if one wishes to avoid taking sides, perhaps it served both purposes.

Whatever was affecting the people now seems to have caused life in small villages to be less desirable for as we move farther into the Great Pueblo period we see the pueblos increase in size. It is true that some small pueblos were still in use but one of the outstanding characteristics of the period was the concentration of the population in pueblos of great size.

An excellent example of this concentration is to be seen in the great Montezuma Valley which lies to the north and west of the Mesa Verde. At an earlier date the Pueblo Indians who occupied this valley lived in many small villages. During the Great Pueblo period the people seem to have banded together to form large communities. A number of enormous pueblos were constructed and in many cases they were built around the springs which supplied water for the populace.

In the Mesa Verde the trend was the same. At the beginning of the period the people lived in numerous small pueblos. After a time they began to band together and toward the end of the twelfth century large pueblos were being built on the mesa tops and in the broad, shallow drainages at the heads of canyons. In some cases several small pueblos were built close together while in other cases several small pueblos were clustered around one or more large ones.

The next change was the most radical of all. About 1200 A. D., the people began to desert the mesa tops and within a short time cliff dwellings were built in almost every cave in the Mesa Verde. Shallow caves were available in great numbers for the mesa contains a score of large canyons. The exact number of cliff dwellings is not known but probably there are as many as six or eight hundred in the canyons of the Mesa Verde.

The events of the Great Pueblo period seem to indicate that the people were faced with some danger which was not present during the earlier periods. The change from small to large pueblos indicates a need for security and the final move to the caves must indicate a definite need for defense. Hundreds of the caves were high on the cliff faces and many of them were additionally fortified with defensive walls.

There can be little doubt that during this period the security of the people was threatened. Now we come to the most difficult question of all. Who was the enemy? Against whom were the people defending their homes? The complete answer is not known but there appear to be two possibilities.

It has been suggested that during this period dissension arose within the Pueblo group itself and the people began to war against each other. This theory will be difficult to prove and events of the period seem to argue against it. If the need for defense resulted from trouble within the tribe one might well expect the people to scatter even more widely with groups leaving the heavily populated areas to seek safety in isolation. But the people did just the opposite. Large areas were deserted and the population became more concentrated than in any previous period.

Four small cliff dwellings with excellent defensive locations

This drawing together of the Pueblo people may well indicate that the threat was from the outside and it is possible that at this time nomadic Indians entered the area and began to harass the farmers. Ceaseless raids of nomadic marauders would exert tremendous pressure on a farming population and withdrawal from the border lands and concentration in certain favorable areas probably indicates a need for defense against an outside enemy.

In 1540, when the Spaniards entered the Southwest, several tribes of nomadic Indians were warring on the Pueblo people and the population had dropped radically. When the Pueblo population was at its height there were hundreds, perhaps thousands, of villages but when the Spaniards came they found less than eighty villages of Pueblo Indians and these were concentrated in a small area in what is now New Mexico and Arizona. Even after the Americans came the population continued to dwindle. Finally there were fewer than thirty villages of Pueblo Indians. Much of this loss of population was due to the harassing activities of nomadic Indians and it is possible that in the Mesa Verde area this trouble began about 1100 A. D.

The identity of the nomadic tribes which warred on the people of the Mesa Verde region is not known. It has been suggested that the early Apaches or the early Utes may have entered the area at that time but there is little positive evidence. Further research may provide an answer to the problem but it is possible the identity of the "enemy people" will never be known.

The Great Pueblo period came to an end just before 1300 A. D., and that is the time when the Pueblo Indians moved away from the Mesa Verde, never to return. As was mentioned in an earlier chapter the Pueblo Indian occupation of the Mesa Verde came to an end during the great drought of 1276 - 1299 A. D. Rainfall was deficient during this period of twenty-four years and before normal weather returned in the year 1300, all of the people had drifted off to the south. Nothing has been found to indicate that the Mesa Verde region was ever occupied by farming Indians after the drouth.

Since the area was deserted during the drouth it is only reasonable to assume that this period of abnormally dry weather was the cause of their leaving. There is much, however, to indicate that the drouth was not the sole cause. During their long occupation of the Mesa Verde the Indians had survived many long periods of drouth. Dry years were not a new experience and they were wise in the ways of existing through unfavorable periods. It is doubtful whether the drouth, severe as it was, would have caused complete abandonment of so large an area. We may feel sure that during the Great Pueblo period a very real danger threatened the people. They moved to the caves, certainly because of a need for security, and the population diminished. Before the drouth came the people were already moving to the south and it is probable that the abnormally dry period simply hastened a movement that was already underway. While the final, complete desertion of the area may be blamed on the drouth it appears that the danger which had threatened for more than a century had much to do with the abandonment of the once populous area.

When normal weather returned in the year 1300, there were no Pueblo Indians in the Mesa Verde. All had perished or had drifted away and the villages were empty and silent. Slowly the centuries paraded by. Drifting earth and vegetation crept over the mesa-top pueblos and the leveling forces of nature caused the once proud cliff dwellings slowly to bow their heads.

Then suddenly the silence of six centuries was broken and the emptiness was gone. Men of a new race came upon the scene and the modern world learned of the glorious past of the Mesa Verde.